W9-ABT-598

# AN ESSAY ON TYPOGRAPHY

| DATE DUE | RETURNED |
|---|---|
| OCT 1 8 2008 | |
| NOV 0 1 2008 | NOV 0 1 2008 |
| SEP 3 0 2009 | OCT 0 1 2009 |
| FEB 0 8 2010 | |
| OCT 0 4 2010 | SEP 2 7 2010 |
| OCT 1 1 2011 | OCT 2 4 2011 |
| MAR 1 5 2012 | MAR 3 0 2012 |
| | |
| | |
| | |
| | |
| | |
| | |
| | |

# AN ESSAY ON TYPOGRAPHY

by

## ERIC GILL

*160201*

With a new introduction by
Christopher Skelton

DAVID R. GODINE, PUBLISHER
BOSTON

PUBLISHING HISTORY

The 1936 edition of *An Essay on Typography* by Eric Gill,
of which this edition is a photo-lithographic copy, was
re-set with extensive changes from the first 1931 edition.
It is set in Joanna, one of the first typefaces designed
by Eric Gill, in 1930, and first used in
*An Essay on Typography*.

For the 1936 edition the original foundry type was used,
cut by H. W. Caslon and Co. Ltd., handset by Hague and Gill
in 12 point with 3 point leading, and printed by them at Pigotts.
The book was published by Sheed and Ward.

The new Introduction to this edition by Christopher Skelton
has been filmset in Linotron 202 10 on 13 point Joanna.

First U.S. Edition published by
DAVID R. GODINE, PUBLISHER, INC.
Post Office Box 450
Jaffrey, New Hampshire 03452
*www.godine.com*

This edition published in the United Kingdom by
Lund Humphries, Limited, London.

ISBN 0-87923-762-7 (HC) / ISBN 0-87923-950-6 (SC)
Library of Congress Catalogue Card Number 88-45284

Fourth softcover printing, 2007
Printed in the United States of America

# INTRODUCTION

The Monotype Corporation exhibition held to celebrate Gill's work in 1958 was called 'Eric Gill: Master of Letters' and it is in that capacity that he is best remembered today.

Although highly regarded as a teacher in the workshop by his assistants and associates his work left him little time for formal teaching. The *Essay on Typography* is the one book that he devoted to any practical aspect of his work with letters. For this reason alone it is worth our continued attention, even though in the thirty-three years since it was last reprinted the revolution in the techniques of the reproduction of letters has been immense. The letters, including Gill's, are still the same as in 1931.

Gill himself defines typography as 'the reproduction of letters by means of movable types', a definition that can include all forms of typesetting and printing although in Gill's context he takes typography as being synonymous with letterpress printing.

The book was first published by Sheed & Ward in 1931, titled on the front of the jacket 'Printing & Piety' and simply 'Typography' on the spine. 'An Essay on Typography' appears on the contents page, which also serves as a title-page. 'Essay' is a misleading description for a work of over 140 pages divided into nine chapters. (It may have been originally intended as a shorter work as René Hague's estimate was for 80 pages of composition.) It was the first substantial piece of Gill's writing to be published. His previously printed works are all small pamphlets, short essays and lectures – mostly collected in *Art Nonsense* in 1929.

Gill began designing typefaces in 1925. Gill Sans was first shown by the Monotype Corporation in 1929, and the first book printed in Perpetua also appeared in that year. Gill's collaboration with Robert Gibbings, begun several years earlier, was at its most active with the drawings for the Golden Cockerel type in 1929 and with *The Four Gospels*, published in 1931. The drawings for the Joanna typeface were started in April 1930. This was the period, too, of Gill's closest association with Stanley Morison, whose *First Principles of Typography* were published in 1930 in *Fleuron* VII. A large part of that volume is devoted to Gill's work. By 1931 he was a considerable figure in the typographical world.

Gill had moved to Pigotts in Buckinghamshire from Capel-y-ffin in South Wales in 1928. In April 1930 he and his future son-in-law, René Hague, set about buying the equipment for the printing business, Hague & Gill, which was to share the farm buildings with the stonecarving workshop and the engraving studio. One of the objects of the new press was to make use of Gill's types and Joanna was designed specifically and exclusively for it. René

Hague, a somewhat wayward Irishman, had met the Gill family in Wales in 1924 and married Gill's daughter, Joanna, after whom the type was named, in November 1930. How he came by his printing knowledge is somewhat obscure although there is no doubting his competence. It may well be that Gill's establishment of this new venture had a lot to do with giving his son-in-law employment within the workshop milieu.

With the years of his type designing coming to fruition, and the establishment of the printing business, it was natural for Gill to set down his ideas on typography in a way that was characteristic of him. The *Essay* can be seen partly as an attempt to explain his excursion into the industrial activity so alien to his often stated principles.

Gill's diary records that he began writing *Typography* in October 1930 while he was in hospital. The writing continued throughout October and November, sometimes being dictated to René Hague. He notes several periods of discussion with him and it is probable that in the more technical sections the book is partly Hague's. Hague himself wrote very little on the subject. His provocative essay 'Reason and Typography'* is full of phrases that echo Gill, and there is no doubt that in typographical matters the two men thought alike.

As we have seen, this was a period of concen-

* *Typography* No 1 (Nov. 1936)

trated activity for Gill. Besides the work mentioned he was busy with drawing the variations of Perpetua and Gill Sans, the BBC carvings and the *Four Gospels* engravings. He seems to have induced activity in others as well: there were barely six months between finishing the drawings for Joanna Roman in June 1930, and his record of correcting the proofs of *Typography* on 4 January 1931. In this time the typefounder, H. W. Caslon, had cut the punches and cast the type, and Hague & Gill had set it up by hand for its first use in the book.

The first edition of 500 copies is noted as no. 4 of the publications of Hague & Gill and is dated in the colophon, June 1931, although Gill's diary records their being signed in September. The whole edition is signed by both Gill and Hague (Hague first). It is printed on the specially watermarked Hague and Gill hand-made paper in a format of 7¾ × 5 inches.

The second edition, which is used for this facsimile, was published in 1936, also by Sheed & Ward, in a smaller format. It has additions to the introductory paragraphs, a new chapter at the end, and other revisions. It is basically the same typesetting as the earlier printing with several significant differences. Joanna italic became available in 1931 and is used for the captions and running headlines. A third edition was published by J. M. Dent & Son in 1941 from the same typesetting (Dents were part owners of Hague & Gill from 1936). The book was reissued by Dents in 1953, but set in the 11 point version of the type that was cut by the Monotype Corporation in 1937.

Sheed & Ward, the book's first publishers, normally handled work of specifically Roman Catholic interest; and from its inception Gill must have regarded the book as something far different from a mere treatise on typography. Underneath the heading 'PRINTING & PIETY' on the jacket of the first edition is the subtitle 'An Essay on life and works in the England of 1931, and particularly TYPO/GRA/PHY', the last word dominating the cover in large red capitals split into three lines. Clearly, it was never intended to be all typography. Although this theme is restated in the opening sentence of the book, the tone and hectoring style of the first chapter must have come as a surprise to those seeking instruction on typographical matters and unfamiliar with Gill's brand of Christian socialism, particularly without the jacket of the first edition to sound a warning.

In the expanded introduction to the 1936 edition Gill wrote, referring to the earlier issue, 'It was one of the author's chief objects to describe two worlds – that of industrialism and that of the human workman – & to define their limits'. It is with the application of his 'two worlds' theory to the trade of printing that the first chapter is especially concerned. 'On the one hand is the world of mechanised industry claiming to be able to give happiness to men and all the delights of human life – provided we are content to have them in our spare time and

do not demand such things in the work by which
we earn our livings', and 'On the other . . . a world
in which the notion of spare time hardly exists, for
the thing is hardly known and very little desired; a
world wherein the work is the life & love accompanies it.' Gill, himself, in the same 1936 introduction
considered that these 'chief objects' had been
'imperfectly remembered' and faulted the book on
that account, although the theme recurs frequently
in succeeding chapters.

He had earlier written essays on stonecarving and
wood-engraving. Those, unlike *Typography*, were
solely concerned with assessing the position of the
practitioner of those arts in twentieth-century society. There is no practical advice in either. In the
typography essay he is ever willing to leave the
practical point to draw a social or religious moral.
Perhaps under the influence of René Hague he was
persuaded to devote more space than he intended
to the chapters on the sound common sense of the
practice of typography, for which the work is chiefly
remembered.

The chapter on lettering is by far the longest in the
book. A historical survey is followed by a discussion
of legibility and letter forms, plain and fancy. The
world of machinery and standardised production
'can only decently turn out the plainest of plain
things', and 'Fancifulness is therefore within the
competence of a smaller and smaller number of

workmen.' Thus it should be with letters. In 1929 Gill himself had designed a fanciful letter, a floriated initial N for Stanley Morison's *Fleuron*. Morison wanted him to design a whole alphabet, but Gill declined, taking the position outlined above that the mechanical methods employed by the Monotype Corporation were in contradiction to the nature of his design. He must have changed his mind by 1936 when Monotype Gill Floriated was made as a complete titling alphabet.

The section headed *Typography* opens with a practical explanation of the application of lettering to printing, roman and italic alphabets, etc. and their uses. His advice on the use of italics would find little support today, least of all his suggestion that for emphasis letter-spaced lower case might be used as a substitute for italics. Nothing is said about the use of small capitals and Gill did not design any for Joanna. He did, however, provide two sets of roman capitals for the face and their use is well demonstrated in the book's pages, the smaller being used generally and the larger for paragraph openings and chapter titles. The height of these 'smaller' capitals is one of the distinguishing and distinguished features of the Caslon cutting of Joanna and contributes to its even appearance on the page.

The 'two worlds' theme then reasserts itself, – 'The typography of industrialism' and 'humane typography'. The latter is comparatively 'rough and uncouth'. One wonders if Gill had in mind the St Dominic's Press and their early printing of his pamphlets and engravings; the word 'humane' then becomes very apposite.

The colophon to the first edition reads: 'Printed by René Hague and Eric Gill'. Was Eric Gill ever a printer? In the sense that he set type and fed sheets of paper into a machine the answer is certainly 'No'. Neither his diary nor his account sheets show any evidence of time spent in this way except briefly with Hilary Pepler at Ditchling in the early years. He certainly printed his own editions of engravings on both wood and metal, using the hand-press in his own workshop. His contribution to the books of Hague & Gill was as typographical advisor; occasional author (the fee he asked for *Typography* was £35); and, as existing records show, financial supporter until 1936.

In Gill's account of machine punch-cutting he is at pains to point out how many different people are involved, another of his habitual disparagements of the industrial system. The earlier essay on wood engraving makes the same point, about mechanical engraving: 'degradation is inevitable when one man draws, another touches up the drawing, another photographs, another touches up the negative,' and so on, until 'to crown all, another takes the profits.'

The short chapter on paper and ink reads strangely in the printing world of today with its talk of hand-made paper and hand-ground ink. Yet even here there are nuggets of sound advice and guiding principles for today's 'humane' printers.

It is perhaps for Gill's advocacy of 'unjustified' setting that *Typography* is best known – that is, pages of typesetting in which the spaces between the words are all even so that as a consequence the lines themselves are of slightly different lengths, resulting in a 'ragged' right-hand margin. The case for close word-spacing has long since been recognised but even today Gill's words are relevant, when the 'tyrannical insistence upon equal lengths of lines' is as much in evidence and when the designer's grid has taken the place of what Gill's chapter heading calls, 'The Procrustean Bed' of the composing stick. Although Gill's remarks are mainly aimed at book designers it is, perhaps, newspaper and advertising typesetters who would most benefit from his advice. The pages of *Typography* itself are, of course, witness to Gill's principles. The first two pages of the chapter are in normal 'justified' setting to demonstrate the argument.

The frequent use of ampersands and the occasional contractions such as 'tho'' and 'sh'ld' may jar, though not as much as one practice abandoned in the 1936 printing shown here. In the first edition the final few letters of some words were set in a smaller size in order to fit them into the line, a very time-consuming practice when hand-setting. Although technically feasible using Monotype hot-metal machine composition and now easily achieved with film-setting, it remains a distracting way to achieve equal word spacing. The use of paragraph marks instead of indented lines, although idiosyncratic today, has distinguished precedents and adds to the evenness and consistency of the pages.

Much unjustified typesetting today is ruined by the unwillingness of the typesetter to break words, resulting in the ugliness of excessively uneven lines. In the use of word breaks and slight adjustments of spacing to achieve not too disparate line lengths Gill's pages are exemplary. This effect, it must be admitted, has been achieved at a cost. Excessively uneven word-spacing is bad, of course, and Gill's cure is effective; but there are just as many word breaks as in normal setting, some of them very dubious. If Gill had used the same treatment with justified setting, one wonders whether any unevenness of word spacing would be noticeable.

It was surely under Gill's influence that the pages of the Golden Cockerel Four Gospels were set with ragged right-hand edges in 1930. The first specimens, which Robert Gibbings favoured, are set normally.

Gibbings and Gill, in their notable collaboration over the Four Gospels must have frequently discussed typographical matters. Of the other influences on Gill's and Hague's typographical ideas it is hard to be certain. There was little in the way of style books and works on typographical design available at the time. De Vinne's volume on composition in the four volume *The Practice of Typography*, full of sound detail, was probably known to them. Morison regarded it highly. His *First Principles of Typography* must have been well known to Gill.

'The workman should not have to watch his instrument, his whole attention should be given to the work.' Thus, under the heading of 'The Instrument' Gill chooses a hand press for the 'humane printer'. He acknowledges the world of the 'automatically fed power presses' and is content to grant each of the two worlds its place. Like much of the rest of the book the pages where Gill writes of printing machines are a kind of charter for his own printing and, incidentally, for the 'fine printer' and small press of today.

What was originally the final section is headed 'The Book'. Gill's logical common sense and practical instruction are to the front as he discusses type sizes, book sizes and margins. There is much good stuff for the book designer and especially healthy advice for those tempted into the current fashion for overdesign and bogus refinement. The title page of the 1936 edition, reproduced in the following pages only partially follows his own advice. It shares the first page of the book with the contents and the publisher's name. The first edition more faithfully reflects Gill's tenets. The title and author's name are no more than a heading to a few lines listing the contents on the opening page. The publisher's name appears on the jacket only.

The final chapter, a substantial addition to the first edition, is really an appendix, in which Gill gives full rein to a hobby horse mounted briefly in the opening paragraph of the 'Typography' section. It is a typical Gill polemic in support of shorthand or what he calls 'phonography', full of sweeping statements, question-begging arguments and pretended naivety ('although the saying "time is money" is too difficult for me to understand'). He calls for the abolition of lettering as we know it and for the substitution of phonographic symbols. So the essay subsides into a thought-provoking and interesting note of crankiness, seeing phonography as a way to start again and rid ourselves of the world of fancy lettering.

*An Essay on Typography* is quintessential Gill. It epitomises his idealism, his pragmatism and his Christian view of the world of everyday work. Practical advice is shot through with moral precept and maxims of wisdom. Parallels are drawn between plain and ornamental lettering and the vicissitudes of Christian marriage, mention of the grinding of ink leads to an extolling of the virtues of pain and suffering. He hardly ever resists an aside critical of commercial activity, often unfair, 'designers who for some inscrutable reasons must live'. It is thus, however, that the reader is stimulated in all sorts of ways other than typographical.

*August 1988*                                    C.S.

# AN ESSAY ON TYPOGRAPHY

## BY ERIC GILL

Contents:

Printed and Made in Great Britain
by Hague & Gill, High Wycombe

Published by
Sheed and Ward
31 Paternoster Row, London E.C.

First Published in 1931
Second Edition 1936

# THE THEME

¶ The theme of this book is Typography, and Typography as it is affected by the conditions of the year 1931. The conflict between industrialism & the ancient methods of handicraftsmen which resulted in the muddle of the 19th century is now coming to its term.

¶ But tho' industrialism has now won an almost complete victory, the handicrafts are not killed, & they cannot be quite killed because they meet an inherent, indestructible, permanent need in human nature. (Even if a man's whole day be spent as a servant of an industrial concern, in his spare time he will make something, if only a window box flower garden.)

¶ The two worlds can see one another distinctly and without recrimination, both recognising what is good in the other — the power of industrialism, the humanity of craftsmanship. No longer is there any excuse for confusion of aim, inconsistency of methods or hybridism in production ; each world can leave the other free in its own sphere.

¶ Whether or no industrialism has 'come to stay' is not our affair, but certainly craftsmanship will be always with us — like the poor. And the two worlds are now absolutely distinct. The imitation 'period work' and the imitation handicrafts merchants alone are certainly doomed. Handicrafts standards are as absurd for mechanised industry as machine standards are absurd for the craftsman.

¶ The application of these principles to the making of letters and the making of books is the special business of this book.

¶ This book was written in 1930, and now that a second and cheaper edition is called for it seems desirable to re-write a great part of it. It was one of the author's chief objects to describe two worlds — that of industrialism and that of the human workman — & to define their limits. It is one of the book's chief faults that that object was but imperfectly remembered. It has not been possible to correct this, but the book has been amended in many small particulars and a chapter added.

¶ Six years is a considerable time in human life, and if it be true that the witty remarks one makes at a dinner party seem peculiarly foolish the next morning, how much more does the enthusiasm of 1930 appear foolish in 1936. The two worlds are still

with us; the industrial world continuing in its diabolical direction, the humane world indestructible
by its very nature. But the divorce between them is
even more complete, and the sphere of the handicraftsman even more curtailed.

¶ The determination to have all necessary things
made by machinery, & to organise machine industry in such a way as to have only a few hour's work
per day is now much more clearly defined than it
was even six years ago. And printing is one of the
obviously necessary things, & to do it in any other
way than by machinery appears more and more
absurd. Thus one after the other the crafts, which
were formerly the workman's means to culture, are
being mechanised more or less completely, & now
only such things as musical composition & painting
pictures & giving lectures on the wireless, demand
the actual responsible skill of the human being who
does them. All other workmen are released from
any other considerations but economic ones. It was
possible to say these things six years ago; but to-day
many more people are conscious of their truth. The
newspapers are full of evidences that people are
beginning to see the issue clearly. The widespread
propaganda of financial reform is alone evidence of

a great change in people's minds. They see now very clearly that the old man of the sea is a financial rather than a social tyrant.

¶ The industrial world may be wrecked by its bad finance and the wars which bad finance foments, or, as seems less likely, a brave new world of logic-ally organised machine production may be achieved. In either case human communications will continue, printing will still be called for, & much in this book may still be useful.

# I. COMPOSITION OF TIME AND PLACE

¶ Time & place must be taken into consideration in the discussion of any human affair, and this is particularly true in an abnormal time like the 20th century. It is not our business to write at length of this abnormality, but it is necessary at least to describe it, though, as is very often the case, it is more easy to say what it is not than what it is. It is not simply that abnormality which is caused by an excess of riches among the few and the poverty of the many; such an excess on either side does not necessarily destroy or disturb the essential humanity of our life. Nor is it the case of a free minority as against an enslaved or servile majority. Such a state may be ethically good or bad, but neither the free nor the slaves are necessarily condemned to a life contrary to nature. The abnormality of our time, that which makes it contrary to nature, is its deliberate and stated determination to make the working life of men & the product of their working hours mechanically perfect, and to relegate all the humanities, all that is of its nature humane,

b

to their spare time, to the time when they are not at work.

¶ The full force of this abnormality is not apparent to the majority; perhaps no more than ten people in England see it. This state of affairs, though now deliberately fostered and definitely stated in many places, has been very gradually arrived at — it is only recently that it has arrived at any sort of completeness; but it is now almost complete and has come to be regarded as in no way contrary to nature and actually to be a normal state of affairs.

¶ This is not the place to demonstrate the steps by which the world has come to such views & to such a condition, nor to discuss the ethical causes and consequences. It is sufficient for our purpose to describe the world of England in 1931, & it is necessary to do that in order that we may see what kind of world it is in which the thing called Typography now exists.

¶ We are concerned with Typography in England; it may be that the conditions are much the same in France, Germany and America, but we have no means of being certain of this. Moreover there are differences of language and even of lettering which make it necessary to restrict the circle in order to avoid confusion. ¶ What sort of a place, then, is England? It should now be possible to describe England pretty clearly; the transition from a preindustrial, agricultural state is now mentally and practically complete; the thing can now be seen sharply defined against the background of her past. There are still all sorts of survivals, and even vigorous survivals, many of which are of their nature permanent and indestructible, but they are to be seen now as survivals and relics and not as integral parts of the world we have made. They are not of the soul of the existing structure, they are bodily survivals determined by another soul. ¶ The small shopkeeper, for instance, is still with us, and though the time has almost come wherein he will have no apparent place, nevertheless his survival is permanent; for nothing can stop small boys from selling one another marbles, and it is that personal dealing which is the root of all trading. ¶ Even the small craftsman, in spite of the impossibility of competition with 'big business' and mass-production, cannot be permanently put out of action, if only because the pen-knife is always with us and men will always want to make things to please themselves, tho' only in their spare time.

¶ Nothing will stop men singing or making songs, even though music 'on tap' supply the bulk of the demand. ¶ And, most important of all, religion, which in spite of its establishment has now no effect in politics, cannot be destroyed. Even tho' every institutional religion be banished from the state, every man will make a religion for himself, for no man can avoid some attempt at an answer to the question 'What's it all blooming well for?'.

¶ Nevertheless, in spite of their indestructibility, these things and others are now to be seen simply as survivals from our pre-industrial past; for industrialism is of its nature inimical to all of them, & it is industrialism that is the body of our modern world. As to its soul we are not immediately concerned; our business is to describe England in that aspect of it which concerns us as producers, makers of things. The spiritual and political description is outside our competence. Mr Maritain, in his recent essay on Religion and Culture, says: 'The modern world is spiritually dominated by the humanism of the Renaissance, the Protestant Reformation and the Cartesian Reform'. And though this be the exact truth its demonstration is here no affair of ours. ¶ Such demonstration, however,

is quite unnecessary, for there are now few who
would wish to deny it. Leaders of shop-keepers,
like Mr Selfridge, or of manufacture like Messrs
Robinson and Cleaver of Belfast (who in their cata-
logues state that they are able to supply 'Best blankets at 80s per pair, blankets 'for the spare room'
at 65s, blankets 'for servants' bedrooms' at 25s,
and blankets 'for charitable purposes' at 18s — or
some such scale of figures), leaders of finance like
Lord Melchett, or of politics like the first Earl of
Birkenhead, would all heartily agree that such are
the spiritual dominations of the modern world.
Here, therefore, we are concerned merely with
description and not at all with either history or
proofs. Almost for the first time we find ourselves
able to say things with which nearly everyone
will agree.

¶ We ask then again: What sort of a place is modern England? As we have said, Religion counts, the
Churches are powerful forces; Nationality counts,
the War could not have been fought had not the
various peoples been moved by notions of patriot-
ism. Customs, habits, all count; the clothes we
wear, the language we speak, our architecture,
tho' for the most part a jumble of all the styles on

earth, all these things count, but as yet they are very little outwardly the product of that which is the essence of our world. ¶ The world is not yet clothed in garments which befit it; in architecture, furniture, clothes, we are still using and wearing things which have no real relation to the spirit which moves our life. We are wearing and using them simply because we are accustomed to them. The intellectual excitement which moves individual designers does not affect the mass of people. The majority still think Gothic architecture to be appropriate to churches, tho' Gothic architecture is simply a method of building appropriate to stone and is not really more Christian than Hindu. We still make tables and chairs, even when we make them by machinery, with the same ornamental turnings & cornices & so forth as when furniture-making was the job of a responsible handicrafts-man. We still wear collars and ties, whether we be kings, clerks or furnace men, though there is no necessity for a collar or a tie in any of these trades. All this is merely intellectual sloth; nobody can be bothered to live according to reason; there is even a strong national feeling of distaste for any attempt to do so. Doubtless a distrust of human reason is reasonable, but few adventures are more honourable than an attempt to live by it.

¶ Now the chief and, though we betray our personal predilection by saying so, the most monstrous characteristic of our time is that the methods of manufacture which we employ and of which we are proud are such as make it impossible for the ordinary workman to be an artist, that is to say a responsible workman, a man responsible not merely for doing what he is told but responsible also for the intellectual quality of what his deeds effect. That the ordinary workman should or could be an artist, could be a man whom we could trust with any sort of responsibility for the work he does, or proud of anything but that kind of craftsmanship which means skill and attention as a machine operator (and that responsibility is a purely moral one) is an idea now widely held to be ridiculous; and the widespreadness of this opinion proves my point as well as I could wish. When I say no ordinary workman is an artist, no one will say I am lying; on the contrary, everyone will say: Of course not.

¶ Such is the state of affairs, and its consequences should be obvious. That they are not is the cause of the muddle in which manufacture is at present to be found. For in a world in which all workmen but a few survivals from pre-industrial times, a number so small as to be now quite negligible, are as irresponsible as hammers and chisels & tools of transport, it should be obvious that certain kinds of work which were the products proper to men for whom work was the natural expression of their intellectual convictions, needs & sympathies, as it was of those who bought it, are no longer either natural or desirable. If you are going to employ men to build a wall, and if those men are to be treated simply as tools, it is imbecility to make such a design for your wall as depends upon your having masons who are artists. The 19th century architects' practice of designing ornamental walls and drawing out full size on paper every detail of ornament is now at last seen to be ridiculous even by architects; it is now understood that ornament is a kind of exuberance and that you cannot be exuberant by proxy; nineteenth century attempts at so being are desolate, and a world which desires pleasure more than anything else finds itself surrounded by things that please no one but fools.

¶ It is now clearly understood that modern building must not rely upon ornament, it must rely

simply upon grandeur, that is integrity and size.
There are things which can be measured; with
these alone can the modern architect, employing
the modern workman, concern himself. Of beauty
there need be no lack, for the beautiful is that which
pleases being seen, and those things are pleasing
when seen which are as nearly perfect as may be
in their adaptation to function. Such is the beauty
of bones, of beetles, of well-built railway arches,
of factory chimneys (when they have the sense to
leave out the ornamental frills at the top), of the
new concrete bridge across the Rhine at Cologne,
of plain brick walls. ¶ There is nothing specifically
human about such things or in such beauty. They
are not redolent of man's delight in himself or
of his love of God. But that is neither here nor
there. We have elected to order manufacture
upon inhuman lines; why should we ask for
humanity in the product? Whether the present
system will or can endure is simply irrelevant to
this essay. The manifold injustices and miseries
which seem to be its accompaniment may or may
not be inevitable, & in any case are not here our
concern; the conditions under which things are
made, the material conditions, the technical con-

ditions, are alone relevant. We are simply concerned to discover what kind of things can be made under a system of manufacture which, whatever its ethical sanction or lack of sanction, is certainly the system we have, the system of which we are proud and the system few desire to alter.

¶ It is necessary to say a few more words about the word 'artist'. We affirm that the word Art means skill, that a work of art is a work of skill, and an artist one who is skilful at making things. It would appear therefore that all things made are works of art, for skill is required in the making of anything. And in spite of industrialism this remains true. But, as we have said, the ordinary workman has been reduced to the level of a mere tool used by someone else. However much skill he may have in his fingers and conscientiousness in his mind, he can no longer be regarded as an artist, because his skill is not that of a man making things; he is simply a tool used by a designer and the designer is alone the artist. ¶ Another thing that must be made clear is that we are not at all oblivious of the real distinction between what the ordinary person nowadays calls art, and the other things. Picture-painting, sculpture, music, are indeed art par excellence, but that they alone are now called art is not because they alone are or can be art, but because they alone to-day are the work of men not only skilful, and not tools in the hands of another, but workmen responsible for the things they make.

¶ Even those higher flights of human skill, about which the critics make so much trouble, those paintings, sculptures, & compositions of music in which human emotion seems to play so large a part that it seems as though emotion were the substance of such works, even these are things demanding skill in their making, and we prefer to call them 'Fine Art' to distinguish them, rather than to deny the name of Art to things whose primary purpose is to supply merely physical conveniences.

¶ The ordinary workman, then, is not an artist; he is a tool in the hands of another. He is a morally sensitive tool, but now, in spite of the continued survival of the old fashioned workman (tho' such survivals are necessarily becoming rarer in the ranks of ordinary workmen), he is not intellectually sensitive. It is clear, therefore, that no demand must be made upon him which calls for anything but good will. As in architecture it is now recognised that even plain masonry must be left from the saw — a chiselled surface has no longer any value — so in all other works & especially in those of factory production, wherein labour is subdivided as much as possible & the product standardised, everything in the nature of ornament must be omitted and nothing must be put in which is not strictly a logical necessity. Houses, clothes, furniture and all appliances and convenient gadgets must be so made; and this is not because we hate ornament & the ornamental, but because we can no longer procure such things; we have not got a system of manufacture which naturally produces them, and, most important of all, if we insist on the ornamental we are not making the best of our system of manufacture, we are not getting the things which that system makes best. ¶ The process by which a railway locomotive has become the beautiful thing it now is, by which the less ostentatious motor-cars have become objects of delight to those who see them, by which plain spoons and forks achieve that quality of neatness which gives nearly as much satisfaction as the best Queen Anne silver, this process must be welcomed in all other departments of manufacture. And if the human race is really convinced that it cannot forgo ornament and the ornamental it must, for the making of such things, have recourse to those workmen who remain outside the industrial system, painters, sculptors and poets of all kinds, in whatever material they work, whether words or wool, & be prepared to pay highly; for such things cannot be cheap when artists and poets are not ordinary workmen but highly intellectual and self-conscious people. And ornamental typography is to be avoided no less than ornamental architecture in an industrial civilisation.

¶ Let us take it for granted, then, that the ordinary workman is no longer an artist; and further that no operation is to be regarded as one for which the workman is intellectually responsible; such intelligence as he has is to be directed solely to the well-doing of what he is told to do. We may leave it to the directors of industry to see to it that labour be properly subdivided & rationalised in accordance with the dictates of economy; we may leave it to politicians & moralists to see to it that the physical conditions of the workers are hygienic & morally justifiable. We, neither directors of labour nor politicians, are solely concerned with the kind

& quality of the things made. It is no longer per-
missible to design things with no reference but to
our own pleasure, leaving it to engineers to design
machines capable of making them; our business is
now to design things which are suitable for machines
to make. And this is not to say that we accept the
limitations of machines as they are to-day, but that
we accept the limitations of machinery as such.
Moreover, and this is even more important, we are
not saying that the machine is the arbiter in design:
the mind is always that. The shape of A cannot be
changed at the bidding of any machine that is or
could be made. But, taking the shape of A to be
that which the judgement of the mind lays down,
we have to conform it to the nature of the machine,
and not attempt to impose upon mechanical production either those ornamental exuberances which
are natural and proper enough to human beings
working with their hands or those peculiarities of
detail which are proper to the pen, the chisel, and
the graver.

¶ But while it is clear that the determining principle
of an industrial world (what the theologians call
its soul) is such as we have described — the perfection of mechanical manufacture, the obliteration

of all intellectual responsibility in the workman, the relegation of all humane interests to non-working hours & the consequent effort to reduce working hours to a minimum — it is equally clear that the outward appearance of our world shows at present very little of the principle which inspires it. The merest glance at the Fleet Street of 1931 shows how little we have yet put on the garb of an industrialism shorn of pre-industrial enthusiasms. We can still endure, tho' with an increasing sense of their ridiculousness, the imitation gothic Law Courts, the quasi-classical West End branch of the Bank of England and all the gimcrack stucco buildings of the nineteenth century. Even the new building of the news paper called The Daily Telegraph, for all its air of modernity, is only an architectural essay in stone stuck on the front of an iron framework; and the sculptures & ornaments which adorn it show how far we are yet from a complete expression of our belief in mechanical perfection and its functional beauty. It is certain, moreover, that we shall never achieve a complete expression; for, quite apart from our notorious readiness to compromise, the essential inhumanity of industrial methods acts as a tonic to the forces which oppose it. However nearly complete the victory of mechanised industry may be, it can never obliterate the fact of human responsibility, & there will always be many who will choose to be masters of their own work & in their own workshops rather than masters of other men working under sub-human conditions, that is to say conditions which deny them intellectual responsibility.

¶ There are, then, two worlds & these twain can never be one flesh. They are not complementary to one another; they are, in the liveliest sense of the words, mortal enemies. On the one hand is the world of mechanised industry claiming to be able to give happiness to men and all the delights of human life — provided we are content to have them in our spare time and do not demand such things in the work by which we earn our livings; a world regulated by the factory whistle and the mechanical time-keeper; a world wherein no man makes the whole of anything, wherein the product is standardised and the man simply a tool, a tooth on a wheel. On the other is the languishing but indestructible world of the small shopkeeper, the small workshop, the studio and the consulting room — a world in which the notion of spare time hardly exists, for the thing is hardly known and very little desired; a world wherein the work is the life & love accompanies it. ¶ These two worlds are nowhere perfectly exemplified, but both worlds strive to perfect themselves. Nowhere is industrialism complete, but all industrialists and millions of their human tools have the ambition to complete it. Nowhere is there a perfectly humane civilisation, but all who are not enthralled by industrialism desire its perfection. On the one hand is the dream of those who imagine a perfectly organised system of mass production; every article of use made to a good standard pattern; a perfected system of marketing and transport, whether Communist or Capitalist; the hours of labour, both for masters & men, reduced to a few hours a day, & a long leisure time devoted to amusement & love-making, even to the pursuit of the thing which they call Art — it will be encouraged by the state, & doubtless prizes will be offered; moreover, to sit on excellent steel furniture in an equally excellent operating-theatre house and do 'fret' work or modelling in clay or 'water colour painting' with mass-produced water colours will give much amusement to many. Then will be seen the truth of the saying that: Industrial-

c

ism has released the artist from the necessity of making anything useful. On the other hand is the normal life of men, scarred, it is true, by every human weakness and malice, but securely founded upon the responsibility of workmen, whether artists or labourers. In such a world there is plenty of time but none to spare. There is less water colour painting but plenty of love-making. There are no modern conveniences but many babies. There would be no one to build the Forth Bridge but plenty to build houses; and the printing of books would be done slowly & painfully by hand. ¶ All these things are said in amity & not in bitterness. An industrialism which really completes itself will have many admirable and noble features. The architecture of our streets and homes will be plain, but it will not therefore be ugly. There is nothing ugly about an operating-theatre strictly designed for its purpose, and a house or flat designed on the same lines need be neither ugly nor uncomfortable. Cushions and colour are the chief ingredients in the recipe for comfort; and rationality, even though limited to a field which excludes all that is sacred, remains the chief ingredient in the recipe for the making of things of beauty. Moreover, from the Pyramid of

Cheops to the bare interior of Westminster Cathedral (before it was spoilt with marbles and mosaics) ornament has never been a necessity of noble architecture; and plain lettering, when properly chosen and rationally proportioned, has all the nobility of plain words.

¶ Nevertheless, this world, this industrialist world, will never complete itself or achieve its perfection. The good that it offers is a positive good, but it excludes too much. The soul of the ordinary man and woman is full of good will; but good sense, logical intelligence, is too rare. However logical, however beautiful plain things are or might be, they will not satisfy the appetites of normal men and women.

¶ Nor, on the other hand, will the humane world ever be perfected; the temptation to save time and money is too strong. Man's good will is undermined by laziness as well as stupidity; by his appetite for amusement no less than his love of power; by his aggressiveness no less than his acquisitiveness. He is thus an easy prey to the allurements of a scientifically organised industrialism which offers him the whole world to play with and dopes him with the idea that in serving it he is serving his fellow-men.

¶ Therefore industrialism will compromise with

the Humane, and the Humane will dally with industrialism. We shall have machine-made ornament (tho' in the near future there will mercifully be less than in the immediate past) and we shall have motor-buses tearing along country roads. We shall have imitation handicrafts in London shops, & cows milked by machinery even on small farms, and we shall have cottage larders stocked with canned foods.

¶ Nevertheless, the positive good & the positive dignity of industrialism will undoubtedly achieve an almost complete ascendancy in men's minds to-morrow, and this ascendancy will purge even the Humane of its foibles. The two worlds will grow more distinct and will recognise each other without the present confusion. The hard and logical development of industrialism will impose, even upon its enemies, a very salutary hardness and logicality. Fancy lettering will be as distasteful to the artist as it will be to the engineer — in fact it is more than probable that it will be the artists who will give the lead. It has always been so. It is not the artist who is sentimental — it is the men of business and the man of science. Even now there are very few really logical & relentless alphabets

of plain letters in common commercial use in this
country, and they were designed by artists. And
even in that age, six hundred years ago, when the
responsibility of workmen was most widely dis-
tributed, & builders, in the absence of mechanical
appliances, & designers, in the absence of unlimited
and cheap drawing paper, were dependent on the
good sense as much as the good will of the workman, there was a restraint, a science, a logic, which
modern architecture does not rival & which even
modern engineering does not surpass. The parish
church of S. Pierre at Chartres, for example, is the
purest engineering; it is as free from sentimental-
ism & frivolity as any iron-girder bridge of to-day,
but it is the engineering of men raised above themselves by a spiritual enthusiasm, whereas the best
modern egineering is but the work of men sub-
human in their irresponsibility and moved by no
enthusiasm but that of material achievement.
¶ Nevertheless, as we have said, the restraint imposed on modern manufacture and building by
modern industrial conditions imposes itself also
on the work of those who stand outside industrialism. Artists no less than engineers are forced
to question the very roots of workmanship, to

discover the first word, the word that was at the beginning. And we can only pray that those who employ industrial methods of manufacture will pursue those methods to a logical and stern conclusion — thus only can our age leave a monument worthy of its profane genius and mechanical triumph — and that those who refuse the blandishments of power or the ease of irresponsibility will discover that in its ultimate analysis the only justification for human work is an intrinsic sanctity.

## 2 . LETTERING

¶ Letters are signs for sounds. Signs for numbers and other things (like the sign for a dollar) may in practice be included, though they are not strictly letters (except as in Roman or Greek numerals & the letter signs used in Algebra). ¶ Letters are not pictures or representations. Picture writing and hieroglyphics are not letters from our point of view; and tho' our letters, our signs for sounds, may be shown to be derived from picture writing, such derivation is so much of the dim and distant past as to concern us no longer. ¶ Letters are not pictures or representations. They are more or less abstract forms. Hence their special and peculiar attraction for the 'mystical mug' called man. More than most things, letters allow him to consider beauty without fear of what the Home Secretary may think or do. Art and morals are inextricably mixed, but the art of lettering is freer from adulteration than most arts; hence among a highly cultured & rational people like the Chinese the high place of calligraphy and inscription. Among the Chinese, good writing is more highly honoured than painting is with us, as highly perhaps as we honour a successful contraption for boiling soap. ¶ It is a matter of satisfaction, therefore, that, in spite of our preoccupation with merely physical convenience, we have inherited an alphabet of such pre-eminent rationality and dignity as the Roman. A good example is the inscription on Trajan's Column at Rome, of which a plaster cast is in the Victoria & Albert Museum, London. ¶ Lettering is for us the Roman alphabet and the Roman alphabet is lettering. Whatever the Greeks or the Germans or the Russians or the Czecho-Slovaks or other people may do, the English language is done in Roman letters, and these letters may be said to have reached a permanent type about the first century A. D. ¶ Though in the course of the centuries innumerable variations in detail have been made, Roman letters have not changed essentially. Fourteen hundred years after the cutting of the Trajan inscription the tablet in Henry VII's chapel was inscribed, and no Roman would have found any difficulty in reading the letters. Eighteen hundred years after the time of Trajan & four hundred years after Henry VII, Roman letters are still made, and in almost the same way (e. g. the Artillery Monument, Hyde Park Corner).

¶ But, although the Roman alphabet has remained essentially unchanged through the centuries, customs & habits of work have changed a great deal. In the time of the Romans, say A. D. 100, when a man said the word 'letters' it is probable that he immediately thought of the kind of letters he was accustomed to seeing on public inscriptions. Altho' all sorts of other kinds of lettering existed (on wax tablets, on papyrus, &c.) the most common kind of formal lettering was the inscription in stone. The consequence was that when he made letters 'as well as he could' it was the stone inscription letter that he took as his model. He did not say: Such & such a tool or material naturally makes or lends itself to the making of such and such forms. On the contrary, he said: Letters *are* such and such forms; therefore, whatever tools & materials we have to use, we must make these forms as well as the tools and material will allow. This order of procedure has always been the one followed. The mind is the arbiter in letter forms, not the tool or the material. This is not to deny that tools and

(Figure 1 shows brush strokes and pen strokes. An ordinary
pointed brush held vertically to the paper will of its nature
make the strokes shown in the upper part of the figure. The
lower part shows the strokes naturally produced by a broad
pen, that is thick strokes, thin strokes, and gradations from
thick to thin. The engraving is facsimile, & is given to show
not good forms or bad, good letters or bad, but simply the
forms characteristic of the brush and pen.)

materials have had a very great influence on letter
forms. But that influence has been secondary, and

for the most part it has been exerted without the craftsman's conscious intention.

¶ If we admit, as it seems we must admit, that in Roman times the public inscription in stone was the chief model for all forms of letters, we shall expect to find that when they began to make lettering with a pen, on paper or skin, the forms of letters would be imitations of inscription forms; and this is precisely what we do find. A good example is the Vergil in the library of St. Gall, Switzerland. A facsimile may be seen in the Palæographical Society's Publications, Series 1, vol. 2, Pl. 208.

¶ Pen writing, even as late as the fourth century, shows very clearly that the scribe had no idea of inventing 'pen' forms of letters, but was simply making as well as he could with a pen what he conceived to be ordinary lettering. Whether he held the pen one way or the other (so that the thick strokes came vertically or horizontally) makes no difference to the primary intention of the scribe. He was not inventing letters; he was writing forms already invented.

¶ But the influence of the tool employed was very great (see figure 1), & in the course of time, owing to the greatly increased use of writings and the

A A A

A λ a a

A a a

A a a

relative decrease in inscriptions, and owing to the
increase of speed in writing and the prevalence of
hastily scribbled writing, people became familiar

with forms of letters which, tho' meant to be ordinary Roman letters, were considerably different.
¶ Thus in the letter A (see figure 2), to make three
separate strokes of the pen was too much for a
man in a hurry, & two-stroke A's became familiar.

(Figure 2, reading in the customary order, shows (1) the
essential form of A; (2) the same with the customary thick
and thin strokes and serifs as made with a brush; (3) the
same as incised with a chisel; (4) the same made with a
broad pen, three strokes; (4–7) the two-stroke A, as developed between the fourth and fifteenth centuries; (8–10)
sixteenth century writing; (11–13) modern forms of the
same, suitable for type.)

By the seventh century this form was well estab-
lished, and was as much recognisable as A as the
original three-stroke Roman form. ¶ In the same
way, the form of serif which was easy to make in
stone (which is, in fact, the natural way to finish
an incised line neatly) was less natural & less easy
with a pen. Penmen took naturally to leaving them
out whenever their presence seemed unnecessary.
¶ The influence of the tool is perhaps less obvious
in stone inscriptions. Inscription cutting is a slow
job anyway. But certain forms are more difficult to
cut than others, e. g. a thick line meeting another

at an angle, as in the K. The letter-cutter naturally avoids such things. ¶ Again, take the letter G. The evolution of our modern small g is seen to be chiefly due to the prevalence of & consequent familiarity with hastily scribbled forms (see fig. 3). Nevertheless, in no case does the scribe imagine he is inventing a new form; he is only concerned to make well or ill the form with which he is familiar.

¶ By the sixth century a form of writing obviously more natural to penmanship (see British Museum Harl. MS. 1775) had been evolved. And the process continued until all resemblance to the Roman original was hidden (see B. M. Add. MS. 24585).

¶ I am not concerned to describe in detail the history of the process in its technical and economic significance. The point that chiefly concerns me is that, with whatever tools or materials or economic circumstance (that is hurry & expense), the artist, the letter-maker, has always thought of himself as making existing forms, & not inventing new ones. Thus, the Lombards of the fourteenth century did not sit down and invent Lombardic lettering. The Siennese inscription in the Victoria and Albert Museum, dated 1309, is simply a stone version of the pen letters with which the letter-cutter was fami-

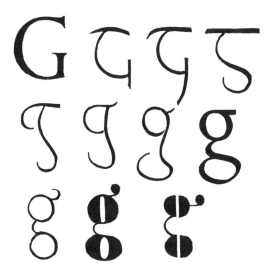

(Figure 3 ( 1 –8) shows the evolution of the lower-case g from the Roman original. 9 – 1 1 are comic modern varieties having more relation to pairs of spectacles than to lettering — as though the designer had said: A pair of spectacles is rather like a g; I will make a g rather like a pair of spectacles.)

liar. The letter-cutters of the fifteenth century did not invent 'gothic'. They had the job of cutting stone inscriptions, and they did it in the ordinary letters of their time. The forms of their letters were what we call 'pen' forms. But they cared nothing about that. To them they were simply letters. And just as we saw that in Roman times the Roman scribe imitated the stone inscription forms because, for him, nothing else was letters; so, in the fifteenth century, when the written was the most common and influential form of lettering, the position is reversed, & the letter-cutter copies the scribe — the stone inscription is imitation pen-writing (with such inevitable small modifications as, in stone, cannot be avoided), whereas in the fourth century the written book was an imitation of the stone inscription (with such small modifications as the pen makes inevitable).

¶ Apart from technical and economic influences the matter is complicated by the differences of individual temperaments and mentalities. Moreover, the physical and spiritual ferment which closed the fifteenth century was accompanied by a revival of interest in and enthusiasm for the things of ancient Greece and Rome, and for the earlier rounder and more legible writing of the ninth & tenth centuries. Nevertheless the first printers were no more the inventors of new letter forms than any other craftsmen had been. The first printed books were simply typographic imitations of pen writing, just as were fifteenth century inscriptions in stone (see fig. 4).

¶ Letters are letters — A is A and B is B — and what we call a gothic A was for Pynson simply A. Print-

ing started in northern Europe, where the gothic
forms were the norm. But the centre of culture was

abcdefghijklmnop
qrstuvwxyz

(Figure 4 : Caslon's Black Letter. This type, like that of
Gutenberg, Caxton, &c., was cut in imitation of fifteenth
century northern European handwriting. But though the
original was handwriting it was for the first printers simply
lettering — the only lettering with which they were familiar,
book-lettering.)

A B C D E F G H I J K L M
N O P Q R S T U V W X Y Z
a b c d e f g h i j k l m n o p
q r s t u v w x y z

(Figure 5 : the Subiaco type. This modern version, cut for
the Ashendene Press, London, of the type of Sweynheim
and Pannartz, 1465, shows the change in style caused by
Italian influence.)

not in the North. German printers moved to the
South. The influence of Italian letter forms may be
d

seen in the 'semi-gothic' or 'semi-humanistic' type
of Sweynheim and Pannartz (see figure 5). Except
in Germany, the gothic forms of letters were generally abandoned. The Italian printers set about the
designing of typographic forms of the round, open
Italian penmanship (see figure 6). Again they did
not invent new forms, but formalised and adapted
existing forms to the exigencies of typefounding
and printing.

A B C D E F G H I J K L M N

O P Q R S T U V W X Y Z

a b c d e f g h i j k l m n o p q

r s t u v w x y z

(Figure 6: Jenson's type. This modern version, cut for the
Cranach Press, Weimar, of the type of Nicolas Jenson,
c. 1490, shows the emancipation achieved both from the
gothic of northern Europe and from handwriting generally.
Henceforth the designing of type was primarily the work
of punch-cutters, that is of engravers. Letters were still
reminiscent but no longer an imitation of handwriting.)

¶ The main work having been done by the early Italian printers, the succeeding centuries saw no great
changes in the forms of Roman type letters. Such

changes as occurred were no longer due to the influence of hand-driven tools like the chisel or the pen, but were due to the varieties of national tem-

# ABCDEFGHIJKLM
# NOPQRSTUVWXYZ
# abcdefghijklmnopqrstu
# vwxyz

Figure 7 : Caslon's Old Face, 1734

# ABCDEFGHIJKLMNOP
# QRSTUVWXYZ
# abcdefghijklmnopqrstu
# vwxyz

Figure 8 : 'Monotype' Bodoni

per & commerce. For instance, it is said that there is something peculiarly English about Caslon's type (figure 7); and, though there is nothing peculiarly

Italian about Bodoni's type (fig. 8), it is clear that
by calling it the first of the modern type faces we
are noting the change of character which we associate with the word 'modernity'. Type faces like
Caslon's, Baskerville's (fig. 9) or Miller & Richard's
Old Style (figure 10) were not assertive enough for
nineteenth century commercial printing. The heaviness, i.e. the absence of much contrast in thick and
thin, of type faces like Jenson's or Aldus's make them
illegible for hurried reading. The needs of commerce
& especially of newspaper printers gave a great im-
petus to the 'modern' type faces. 'Modern face' became the ordinary face, and everything conformed
to it. The nineteenth century letter-cutter, as may
be seen by nineteenth century tombstones, did his
best to do 'modern face' in stone. Engravers & even
the writers of illuminated addresses did the same.
¶ The twentieth century is witnessing a reaction.
It is a multifold reaction, partly intellectual, partly
moral, partly anti-commercial, though commerce
is not behind itself in its effort to extract profit even
from anti-commercialism. The nineteenth century
developed machinery, & machine-makers are now
able to supply accurate, though mechanical, imitations of the type faces of the pre-commercial era.

Letters are letters, whether made by hand or by
machine. It is, however, desirable that modern
machinery should be employed to make letters
whose virtue is compatible with their mechanical

ABCDEFGHIJKLMNO
PQRSTUVWXYZ
abcdefghijklmnopqrstu
vwxyz

Figure 9 : 'Monotype' Baskerville

ABCDEFGHIJKLMN
OPQRSTUVWXY&Z
abcdefghijklmnopqrstu
vwxyz

Figure 10: Miller & Richard's Old Style

manufacture, rather than exact and scholarly resuscitations of letters whose virtue is bound up with their derivation from humane craftsmanship.

¶ While the main stream of lettering has run in typographic channels for the last four hundred years, there has, of course, continued the need of lettering in many other things than books and newspapers. Even handwriting has maintained its existence, & the style of letter called italic still preserves its 'cursive' character. Most italic type faces, however, (see figure 11, 5) are too sloping and too cursive. There is a great need of a narrow and less sloping letter, which, while giving emphasis and difference, shall be of the same noncursive character as the upright letters they are used with. Both the Perpetua (fig. 11, 3) and the Joanna italics (figure 11, 4) are so designed, and the latter having only a very slight slope is used with the upright capitals. The Joanna 'italic' was designed primarily to be used by itself, i. e. as a book face and not simply as a letter to be used for emphasis.

¶ The same excessively cursive quality as afflicts Italic has always afflicted Greek types (fig. 11, 7). For some reason or other, probably the comparative rareness of Greek printing, the leaders of typographic design in the fifteenth century never achieved for Greek what they did for Latin & modern languages. That the thing is possible is shown

ABCDEFGHIJKLMNOPQRSTUVWXYZ

abcdefghijklmnopqrstuvwxyz

*abcdefghijklmnopqrstuvwxyz*

abcdefghijklmnopqrstuvwxyz

*abcdefghijklmnopqrstuvwxyz*

ΑΒΓΔΕΖΗΘΙΚΛΜΝΞΟΠΡΣΤΥΦΧΨΩ

αβγδεζηθικλμνξοπρσστυφχψω

ΑΒΓΔΕΖΗΘΙΚΛΜΝΞΟΠΡΣΤΥΦΧΨΩ

αβγδεζηθικλμνξοπρστυφχψω

(Figure 11 : 1 and 2, Perpetua Roman capitals and lowercase; 3, Perpetua italic; 4, Joanna italic; 5, Caslon Old Face italic; 6 & 7, Porson Greek capitals & lower-case; 8 & 9, Perpetua Greek capitals and lower-case.)

by what the Emperor Peter the Great did in the case of Russian writing. The Russian alphabet is closely related to the Greek. The formalisation of Russian script was achieved very successfully by the Dutch typographers employed by Peter the Great; & the same thing could be done for Greek. ¶ Many varieties of Greek types exist, but for the most part they are more italic than the Italics. In recent years attempts have been made at improvement, but no attempt has been made to take advantage of the fact that Greek capitals have always been made in the same way as Roman capitals. Instead of keeping the capitals as they are and designing a lower-case to match, reformers have always proceeded in the opposite way and altered the capitals to match an improved and less cursive lower-case. The Perpetua Greek (fig. 11, 8 and 9) is the first example of an attempt to do for Greek what Peter the Great did for Russian and Jenson and others did for Latin. Just as the capitals of the Perpetua Greek are of precisely the same family as Perpetua Roman, so the Perpetua Greek lower-case is of the same family as the Perpetua Roman lower-case. The letter & serif formation is uniform throughout. ¶ Letters are letters. A is A, and B is B. The letter-maker of the twentieth century has not got to be an inventor of letter forms but simply a man of intelligence & good will. ¶ Whether in stone, wood, paint or metal

> The common problem, yours, mine, everyone's,
> Is — not to fancy what were fair in life
> Provided it could be — but, finding first
> What may be, then find how to make it fair

& the word fair can be taken in both senses — it means both beautiful and just.

¶ As the Roman, when he thought of lettering, thought of inscription letters; as the medieval man thought of written letters; so in the twentieth century, when we write a letter carefully we call it 'printing'. The printed letter is lettering for us.

¶ But there are many forms of printed letter which do not seem entirely satisfactory. One of the commonest forms of unsatisfactoriness is due to the unnecessary and therefore unreasonable mixing of many different sorts of letters on the same page or in the same book. It is a safe rule not to mix different styles of letters on the same page, or different faces of type in the same book. A book printed in an inferior type will be better if that inferior type be strictly kept to than if other and even better types be mixed in with it.

¶ The business of poster letters (see figure 12) has not yet been extricated from the degradations imposed upon it by an insubordinate commercialism. Mere weight and heaviness of letter ceases to be effective in assisting the comprehension of the reader when every poster plays the same shouting game. A man at whom twenty brick manufacturers throw

# A
# DEMON
# WHO LIVES
# ON THE
# DEAD

(Figure 1 2 is a reduced copy of a 'John Bull' poster. It shows how the desire to arrest attention by making the letters as black as possible defeats the object of the poster, i. e. quick legibility. For from a very short distance the letters are indistinguishable.)

bricks from every side at once is quite unable to distinguish the qualities in which 'Blue Staffordshires' are superior to 'London Stocks'. A return to mere

# A
# DEMON
# WHO LIVES
# ON THE
# DEAD

(Figure 1 3 shows a poster letter designed to give the maximum blackness compatible with quick legibility and a rational differentiation between the letters, e. g. the D & O.)

legibility (see fig. 1 3) seems desirable even if the effect be less striking. To this end it is necessary to study the principles of legibility — the characters which distinguish one letter from another, the proportions of light and dark in letters and spacing.

¶ A square or oblong with its corners rounded off may, by itself, be more like an O (see fig. 14) than anything else, but in conjunction with a D made on the same principles there is not much by which to recognise which is which, and from a distance the two are indistinguishable. Many engineers affect this style of letter, believing it to be devoid of that 'art-nonsense' on the absence of which they pride themselves. That newspaper-vendors should use the same style of letter is even more surprising. If the aims of engineers and newsagents were purely decorative, we could more easily appreciate their efforts, even though, to our more rational minds, names on locomotives and advertisements of the contents of more or less untrustworthy journals seem alike unnecessary.

¶ Legibility, in practice, amounts simply to what one is accustomed to. But this is not to say that because we have got used to something demonstrably less legible than something else would be if we could get used to it, we should make no effort to scrap the existing thing. This was done by the Florentines and Romans of the fifteenth century; it requires simply good sense in the originators & good will in the rest of us. ¶ Good will

seems to be the common possession of mankind,
but its complement, good sense, i.e. intelligence,
critical ability, and that intense concentration
upon precise perfection which is a kind of genius,

(Figure 4: 1 & 2 show the engineers' O & D, hardly
distinguishable from one another; 3 & 4 show forms equally
black, no wider, but more legible, which are suitable where
the space required for the normal, 5 & 6, is not available.)

is not so common. Good will comes from below &
occasionally penetrates into studios and cabinets.
Good sense comes from above & percolates thro'
the mass of people. Everybody thinks that he
knows an A when he sees it (fig. 16); but only the

few extraordinary rational minds can distinguish between a good one & a bad one, or can demonstrate precisely what constitutes A-ness. When is an A not an A? Or when is an R not an R (fig. 17)? It is clear that for any letter there is some sort of norm. To discover this norm is obviously the first thing to be done.

ABCDEFGHIJKLM
NOPQRSTUVWX
Y&Z 1234567890
abcdefghijklmno
pqrstuvwxyz

Figure 15: Monotype sans-serif

¶ The first notable attempt to work out the norm for plain letters was made by Mr Edward Johnston when he designed the sans-serif letter for the London Underground Railways. Some of these letters are not entirely satisfactory, especially when it is remembered that, for such a purpose, an alphabet should be as near as possible 'fool-proof', i.e. the forms should be measurable, patient of dialectical exposition, as the philosophers would say — nothing should be left to the imagination of the signwriter or the enamel plate maker. In this quality of 'fool-proofness' the Monotype sans-serif face (figure 15) is perhaps an improvement. The letters are more strictly normal — freer from forms depending upon appreciation and critical ability in the workman who has to reproduce them.

¶ But, as there is a norm of letter form — the bare body so to say, of letters — there is also a norm of letter clothes; or rather there are many norms according as letters are used for this place or purpose or that. Between the occasion wherein the pure sans-serif or mono-line (block) letter is appropriate & that in which nothing is more appropriate than pure fancifulness (see fig. 17, 9, 13, 15 & 16), there are innumerable occasions.

¶ A typically moral and conscientious Englishman finds it exceedingly difficult to keep morals out of art talk; he finds himself inclined to think, e.g. that R ought to have a bow more or less semi-circular and of a diameter about half the height of the stem, & a strongly outstanding tail; that an R with a very large bow and hardly any tail at all is wrong. But such moral notions as the word 'ought' implies, &

such words as 'right' & 'wrong' — taken as having
a moral connotation — are obviously absurd in such
a discussion, and we should be ready to admit that
any old shape will do to make a letter with. Nevertheless, special circumstances demand special treatment, and as a 'confirmed drunkard' may be well
advised to 'take the pledge' & deck himself out with
blue ribands, so, seeing the whirl of eccentricity into which modern advertising is driving us (fig. 18),

(Fig. 16 : 1, essential form; 2, too narrow; 3 & 4, absurd
misconceptions; 5 & 6, normal; 7, overbold; 8, suitable for
advertisements of 'Bovril'; 9, normal sans-serif; 10, sans
bold; 11, sans overbold; 12, hardly recognisable; 13 & 14,
thick and thin unusually disposed; 15, A undecided as to
whether it is an A or an aitch; 16 and 17, normal; 18, top-
heavy; 19, a decent variation; 20, a poor thing but might
be worse; 21, a fancy possibility; 22, essential form of lower-
case a; 23, normal type form; 24, Victorian vulgarity; 25,
comic variety; 26–29, A's that are not A's.)

it seems good and reasonable to return to some
idea of normality, without denying ourselves the
pleasure and amusement of designing all sorts of
fancy letters whenever the occasion for such arises.
Moreover, it seems clear that as a firm and hearty
belief in Christian marriage enables one not only

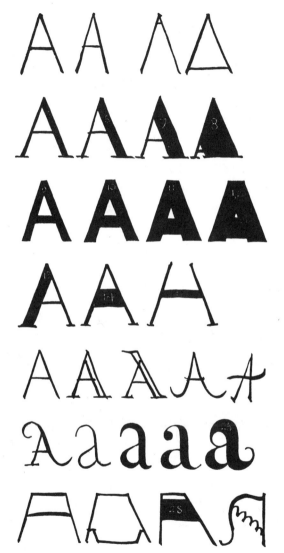

Figure 16

e

to make the best jokes about it but even to break the rules with greater assurance (just as a man who knows his road can occasionally jump off it, where-as a man who does not know his road can only be on it by accident), so a good clear training in the making of normal letters will enable a man to in-dulge more efficiently in fancy and impudence.

(Figure 1 7 : 1, normal sans-serif; 2–5, unseemly abnor-malities & exaggerations; 6, normal with serifs; 7, normal bold; 8, overbold and fatuous; 9–1 3, 1 5 and 1 6, seemly 'fancy' varieties of the normal; 1 4 & 1 7, R's with normal bows but tails badly attached.)

¶ But under an industrial system, such as we have in England to-day, the majority of workmen are de-prived, not by cruel masters, but by the necessary conditions of machine production, of the ability to exercise any fancy or impudence at all, & are even deprived of any appetite so to do. Fancifulness is therefore within the competence of a smaller and smaller number of workmen. We shall shortly have a situation wherein all jokes and eccentricities are the work of 'designers' — and machine-made jokes reproduced by the million tend to be boring. ¶ The kind of figure 2 shown in fig. 1 9, or the r's in fig. 20, with violently contrasted thick & thin forms & enor-

Figure 17

mous blobs might be amusing to meet if they were the unaided efforts of some sportive letter designer. But having become common forms they are about as dull as 'Robots' would be if they all had red noses. As machinery & standardised production can only decently turn out the plainest of plain things, we shall have to steel our minds to a very ascetical and mortified future. This will be quite satisfactory to 'highbrows' like ourselves, but it is certain that the masses of the people will not stand it; & designers, who for inscrutable reasons 'must live', will continue to fall over one another in their efforts to design fancy forms which, like a certain kind of figure 9, are all tail and no body (see figure 19, 24).

¶ However, in spite of industrialism, letter designing is still an occupation worthy of the enthusiasm of rational beings, and, though a Q which were all queue & no Q would be 'past a joke', it is difficult to say exactly where a tail should end (see figure 21). The only thing to do is to make ourselves into such thoroughly and completely rational beings that our instinctive or intuitive reactions and responses and sympathies are more or less bound to be rational also. And just as we revolt from smells which are bad for our bodies without reasoning about it, so

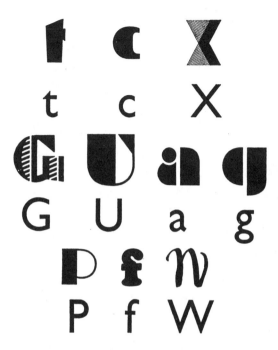

Figure 18

shall we revolt against the mentally defective.
¶ A final word may be said about the influence of
tools in letter designing. The main stream of lettering to-day is undoubtedly the printed sheet or book.
But whatever may be said about the derivation of
our letters from the chisel-made or pen-made letters of the past, there is no doubt whatever that
neither the chisel nor the pen has now any influ-

ence at all. Even the influence of the tools of the punch-cutter is now practically negligible. But a very considerable influence is exerted by the natures of type-metal and type-setting. The short-tailed Q is obviously the result of such influences. Paper also exerts a big influence. The very even & smooth surfaces of modern machine-made papers have given a spur to the designing of type-faces with very finely cut and finished serifs. Influences such as these are obvious, but they are of a very different kind from those exerted by the shapes and usages of chisels and pens.

(Figure 19: 1, 5, 9, 13, 17, and 21, normal forms; the remainder shows various exaggerations; 8 is a common form of vulgarity; 10 & 11 are common misconceptions; 22 and 24 are copies of figures actually seen in advertisements.)

¶ Apart from printing, the lettering of the world is very small in quantity, and therefore such tools as the graver, the brush and the pen and the chisel are negligible, regarded as powers for influencing the forms of letters. The copybook of to-day is the printed page. But this is not to say that one craft should laboriously imitate the technicalities of another, or that small & inessential details which are appropriate in one material should be copied in an-

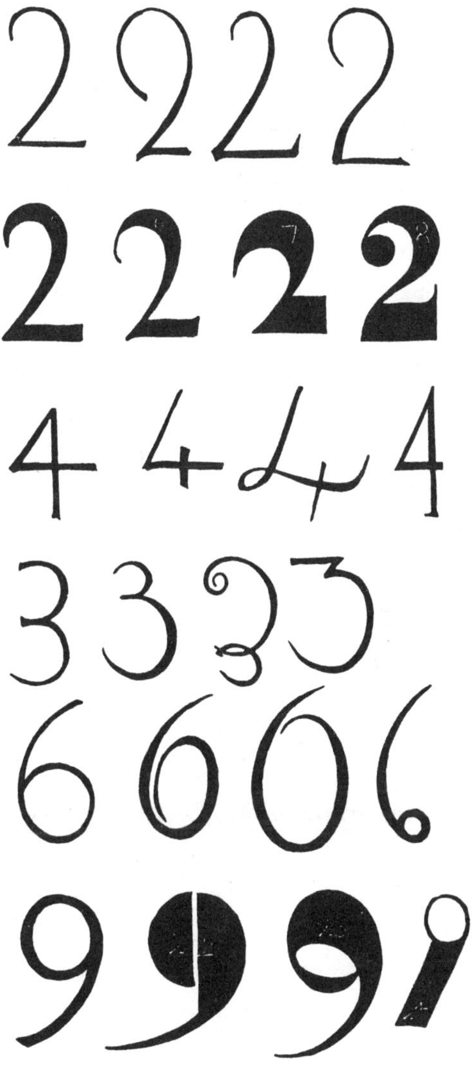

Figure 19

other for which, may be, they are not at all appropriate. It is simply to say that in considering what
forms constitute this or that letter the mind, not
the tool, is the arbiter; and the mind, as regards lettering, is informed by the printed page.

¶ In spite of this we have a tradition of handwriting which seems to pay little or no attention to
either printed or painted letters, & we have copper-
plate engraving of visiting cards and such-like in a
style of lettering only remotely related to typography and apparently quite independent. In all the
various lettering trades there is little or no conscious
reference to printing, & at all times there have been
subsidiary traditions carrying on apparently inde-
pendently of the main stream. Court hands, lawyers' hands, ecclesiastical hands and so forth, have
gone on in their own sweet way without any apparent sign of being influenced by whatever was the
main stream of their time. But this independence is
only apparent. These various by-paths either wan-
der away & are lost, the trades with which they are
connected die out, or the force of the main stream
drags them back. Modern handwriting & copper-
plate printing are both in this predicament. Modern
handwriting, if it is to be reformed at all, must be

# r r r r

(Figure 20 : 1, normal; 2, a possible variety; 3 & 4, Egypt-
ian elephantiasis, commonly seen but uncommonly bad —
except in this diagram.)

(Figure 21 shows various possible varieties of tails.)

reformed by the application of a good knowledge of the technique of penmanship to a knowledge of good printing, & not by the resuscitation of medieval calligraphy. ¶ Modern signwriting & engraving must toe the same line; & in inscription carving, while we may remember Trajan lovingly in the museum, we must forget all about him in the workshop.

(Figure 22 illustrates the contention that slope in either direction does not deprive capitals, lower-case or italics of their essential differences.)

## 3. TYPOGRAPHY

¶ One of the most alluring enthusiasms that can occupy the mind of the letterer is that of inventing a really logical and consistent alphabet having a distinct sign for every distinct sound. This is especially the case for English speaking people; for the letters we use only inadequately symbolise the sounds of our language. We need many new letters and a revaluation of existing ones. But this enthusiasm has no practical value for the typographer; we must take the alphabets we have got, and we must take these alphabets in all essentials as we have inherited them.

¶ First of all, then, we have the ROMAN ALPHABET of CAPITAL letters (upper-case), and second the alphabet which printers call ROMAN LOWER-CASE. The latter, tho' derived from the capitals, is a distinct alphabet. Third we have the alphabet called ITALIC, also derived from the capitals but through different channels. These are the three alphabets in common use for the English people.

¶ Are there no others? It might be held that there are several; there are, for example, the alphabet called Black Letter, and that called Lombardic. But these are only partial survivals, & very few people could, without reference to ancient books, write down even a complete alphabet of either. As far

(Figure 23 : the upper line of letters is essentially 'Roman lower-case'; the lower essentially 'italic'.)

as we are concerned in modern England, Roman capitals, lower-case and italics are three different alphabets, and all are current 'coin'. But however familiar we are with them, their essential differences are not always easily discovered. It is not a

matter of slope or of serifs or of thickness or thin-
ness. These qualities, though one or other of them
may be commonly associated with one alphabet
more than another, are not essential marks of difference. A Roman capital A does not cease to be a
Roman capital A because it is sloped backwards or
forwards, because it is made thicker or thinner, or
because serifs are added or omitted; and the same
applies to lower-case and italics (see figure 22).

¶ The essential differences are obviously between
the forms of the letters. The following letters, a b d
e f g h k l m n q r t u and y, are not Roman capitals,
& that is all about it. The letters shown in the lower
line of fig. 23 are neither capitals nor lower-case.
The conclusion is obvious; there is a complete alphabet of capital letters, but the lower-case takes 10
letters from the capital alphabet, & the italic takes
10 from the capitals and 12 from the lower-case.
Figure 24 shows the three alphabets completed, &
it will be seen that C I J O P S V W X and Z are common to all three, that b d h k l m n q r t u and y are
common to lower-case and italics; that A B D E F
G H K L M N Q R T U and Y are always capitals; &
that a e f and g are always lower-case. ¶ But tho'
this is a true account of the essential differences

between the three alphabets, there are customary
differences which seem almost as important. It is
customary to make Roman capitals upright. It is
customary to make lower-case smaller than capitals when the two are used together; and it is cus-

(Figure 24 shows the differences and similiarities between
the three 'current' alphabets. Note: the curve of the italic
y's tail is due to exuberance, and not to necessity.)

tomary to make italics narrower than lower-case,
sloping towards the right and with certain details
reminiscent of the cursive handwriting from which
they are derived. Fig. 25 shows the three alphabets

(Figure 25 shows the capitals, Roman lower-case and
italics with their customary as well as their essential
differences.)

with their customary as well as their essential differences. ¶ Properly speaking there is no such thing
as an alphabet of italic capitals, and where upright
or nearly upright italics are used ordinary upright

Roman capitals go perfectly well with them. But as italics are commonly made with a considerable slope & cursive freedom, various sorts of sloping & quasi-cursive Roman capitals have been designed to match. This practice has, however, been carried to excess; the slope of italics and their cursiveness have been much overdone. In the absence of punch-cutters with any personal sensibility as letter designers, with punch-cutting almost entirely done by machine, the obvious remedy is a much more nearly upright & noncursive italic, & for capitals the ordinary upright Roman. Even with a nearly upright italic, the mere presence of the italic *a e f* and *g* alters the whole character of a page, & with a slight narrowness as well as a slight slope, the effect is quite different from that of a page of lower-case. ¶ The common practice of using italics to emphasise single words might be abandoned in favour of the use of the ordinary lower-case with spaces between the letters (letter-spaced). The proper use of italics is for quotations & foot-notes, & for books in which it is or seems desirable to use a lighter & less formal style of letter. In a book printed in italics upright capitals may well be used, but if sloping capitals be used they should only be used

as initials — they go well enough with italic lower-
case, but they do not go with one another.

¶ We have, then, the three alphabets, & these are
the printer's main outfit; all other sorts of letters
are in the nature of fancy letters, useful in inverse
proportion to the importance and quantity of his
output. The more serious the class of books he prints,
the wider the public to whom he appeals, so much
the more solemn and impersonal and normal will
be & should be his typography. But he will not call
that book serious which is merely widely bought,
& he will not call that a wide appeal which is made
simply to a mob of forcibly educated proletarians.
A serious book is one which is good in itself according to standards of goodness set by infallible author-
ity, and a wide appeal is one made to intelligent
people of all times and nations.

¶ The invention of printing and the breakdown of
the medieval world happened at the same time;
and that breakdown, tho' hastened by corruption
in the Church, was chiefly caused by the recrud-
escence of a commercialism which had not had a
proper chance since the time of the Romans. The
invention of double-entry book-keeping also happened about the same time, and though, as with
f

modern mechanical invention, the work was done by men of brains rather than men of business, it was the latter who gained the chief advantage. Printing, a cheaper method of reproducing books than handwriting, came therefore just at the right moment. Since its first fine careless rapture, and in spite of the genuinely disinterested efforts of ecclesiastical presses, University presses & the work of many notable individual printers & type-founders, the history of printing has been the history of its commercial exploitation. As is natural with men of business, the worse appears the better reason. Financial success is, rightly, their only aim, and technical perfection the only criterion they know how to apply to their works.

¶ TYPOGRAPHY (the reproduction of lettering by means of movable letter types) was originally done by pressing the inked surface or 'face' of a letter made of wood or metal against a surface of paper or vellum. The unevenness and hardness of paper, the irregularities of types (both in respect of their printing faces and the dimensions of their 'bodies') and the mechanical imperfections of presses and printing methods made the work of early printers notable for corresponding unevennesses, irregularities & mechanical imperfections. To ensure that every letter left its mark more or less completely & evenly, considerable and noticeable impression was made in the paper. The printed letter was a coloured letter at the bottom of a ditch.

¶ The subsequent development of typography was chiefly the development of technical improvements, more accurately cast types, smoother paper, mechanically perfect presses. Apart from the history of its commercial exploitation, the history of printing has been the history of the abolition of the impression. A print is properly a dent made by pressing; the history of letterpress printing has been the history of the abolition of that dent.

¶ But the very smooth paper and the mechanically very perfect presses required for printing which shall show no 'impression' can only be produced in a world which cares for such things, and such a world is of its nature inhuman. The industrial world of to-day is such, and it has the printing it desires and deserves. In the industrial world Typography, like house building & sanitary engineering, is one of the necessary arts — a thing to be done in working hours, those during which one is buoyed up by the knowledge that one is serving one's fellow men, and neither enjoying oneself like an artist nor praising God like a man of prudence. In such a world the only excuse for anything is that it is of service. Printing which makes any claim on its own account, printers who give themselves the status of poets or painters, are to be condemned; they are not serving; they are shirking. Such is the tone of the more romantic among men of commerce; and the consequence is a pseudo-asceticism & a bastard aesthetic. The asceticism is only a sham because the test of service is the profits shown in the accounts; and the aesthetic is bastard because it is not founded upon the reasonable pleasure of the mind of the workman and of his customer, but upon the snobbery of museum students employed by men of commerce to give a saleable appearance to articles too dull otherwise to please even the readers of the Daily Mail. ¶ Nevertheless, as we have already shown, commercial printing, machine printing, industrial printing, would have its own proper goodness if it were studiously plain and starkly efficient. Our quarrel is not with such a thing but only with the thing that is neither one nor the other — neither really mechanically perfect and physically serviceable, nor really a work of art, i.e. a thing made by a man who, however laughable it may seem to men of business, loves God and does what he likes, who serves his fellow men because he is wrapped up in serving God — to whom the service of God is so commonplace that it is as much bad form to mention it as among men of business it is bad form to mention profits.

¶ There are, then, two typographies, as there are two worlds; &, apart from God or profits, the test of one is mechanical perfection, and of the other sanctity — the commercial article at its best is simply physically serviceable and, per accidens, beautiful in its efficiency; the work of art at its best is beautiful in its very substance and, per accidens, as serviceable as an article of commerce.  ¶ The typography of industrialism, when it is not deliberately diabolical & designed to deceive, will be plain; and in spite of the wealth of its resources — a thousand varieties of inks, papers, presses, and mechanical processes for the reproduction of the designs of tame designers — it will be entirely free from exuberance and fancy. Every sort of ornament will be omitted; for printers' flowers will not spring in such a soil, and fancy lettering is nauseating when it is not the fancy of typefounders and printers but simply of those who desire to make

something appear better than it is. Paradoxical tho'
it be, the greater the wealth of appliances, the less is
the power of using it. All the while that the technical
and mechanical good quality is increasing, the de-
humanising of the workmen is also increasing. As
we become more and more able to print finer and
more elaborate & delicate types of letter it becomes
more & more intellectually imperative to standard-
ise all forms and obliterate all elaborations and fancifulness. It becomes easier and easier to print any
kind of thing, but more and more imperative to
print only one kind. ¶ On the other hand, those
who use humane methods can never achieve mechanical perfection, because the slaveries and stan-
dardisations of industrialism are incompatible with
the nature of men. Humane Typography will often
be comparatively rough & even uncouth; but while
a certain uncouthness does not seriously matter in
humane works, uncouthness has no excuse whatever in the productions of the machine. So while
in an industrialist society it is technically easy to
print any kind of thing, in a humane society only
one kind of thing is easy to print, but there is every
scope for variety and experiment in the work itself. The more elaborate and fanciful the industrial

article becomes, the more nauseating it becomes —
elaboration and fancifulness in such things are in-
excusable. But there is every excuse for elaboration
and fancy in the works of human beings, provided
that they work and live according to reason; and it
is instructive to note that in early days of printing,
when humane exuberance had full scope, printing
was characterised by simplicity and decency; but
that now, when such exuberance no longer exists
in the workman (except when he is not at work),
printing is characterised by every kind of vulgarity
of display and complicated indecency.

¶ But, alas for humanity, there is the thing called
compromise; and the man of business who is also
the man of taste, and he of taste who is also man
of business will, in their blameless efforts to earn a
living (for using one's wits is blameless, and earning
a living is necessary) find many ways of giving a
humane look to machine-made things or of using
machinery & the factory to turn out, more quickly
and cheaply, things whose proper nature is derived
from human labour. Thus we have imitation 'period'
furniture in Wardour Street, and we have imitation
'arts & crafts' in Tottenham Court Road. The-man-
of-business-who-is-also-man-of-taste will tend to

the 'period' work, the-man-of-taste-who-is-also-man-of-business will tend to the imitation handicrafts. And, in the printing world, there are business houses whose reputation is founded on their resuscitations of the eighteenth century, & private presses whose speed of output is increased by machine-setting & gas engines. These things are more deplorable than blameworthy. Their chief objectionableness lies in the fact that they confuse the issue for the ordinary uncritical person, and they turn out work which is neither very good nor very bad. 'Period' printing looks better than the usual vulgar products of un-restrained commercialism, and there is no visible difference, except to the expert, between machine-setting and hand-setting, or between sheets worked on a hand press and those turned out on a power-driven platen. ¶ Nevertheless, even if these things be difficult to decide in individual instances, there can be no sort of doubt but that as industrialism requires a different sort of workman so it also turns out a different kind of work — a workman sub-human in his irresponsibility, and work inhuman in its me-chanical perfection. The imitation of the work of pre-industrial periods cannot make any important ultimate difference; the introduction of industrial

methods and appliances into small workshops cannot make such workshops capable of competition
with 'big business'. But while false standards of good
taste may be set up by 'period' work, this 'good
taste' is entirely that of the man of business & his
customers; it is not at all that of the hands — they
are in no way responsible for it or affected by it;
on the other hand, the introduction of mechanical
methods into small workshops has an immediate
effect on the workmen. Inevitably they tend to take
more interest in the machine and less in the work,
to become machine-minders and to regard wages
as the only reward. And good taste ceases to be the
result of the restraint put upon his conscience by
the workman himself; it becomes a thing imposed
upon him by his employer. You cannot see the difference between a machine-set page and one set by
hand. No, but you can see the difference between
Cornwall before and after it became 'the English
Riviera'; you can see the difference between riding
in a hansom & in a motor-cab — between a 'cabby'
& a 'taxi-man'; you can see the difference between
the ordinary issue of 'The Times' to-day and its ordinary issue a hundred years ago; you can see the
difference between an ordinary modern book and

an ordinary book of the sixteenth century. And it is not a question of better or worse; it is a question of difference simply. Our argument here is not that industrialism has made things worse, but that it has inevitably made them different; and that whereas before industrialism there was one world, now there are two. The nineteenth century attempt to combine industrialism with the Humane was necessarily doomed, and the failure is now evident. To get the best out of the situation we must admit the impossibility of compromise; we must, in as much as we are industrialists, glory in industrialism and its powers of mass-production, seeing that good taste in its products depends upon their absolute plainness and serviceableness; and in so much as we remain outside industrialism, as doctors, lawyers, priests and poets of all kinds must necessarily be, we may glory in the fact that we are responsible workmen & can produce only one thing at a time.

¶ That if you look after goodness and truth beauty will take care of itself, is true in both worlds. The beauty that industrialism properly produces is the beauty of bones; the beauty that radiates from the work of men is the beauty of holiness.

## 4. PUNCH-CUTTING

¶ There are two ways of cutting punches — by hand and by machine.

¶ Cutting a punch by hand means cutting on steel, with the appropriate gravers, chisels, or other tools, an exact model of the letter or other symbol in the mind of the punch-cutter or the designer for whom he is working. In addition to the 'face' of the letter (i.e. the actual printing surface of the punch), the punch-cutter is responsible for the right shaping of the punch seen in section. The 'bevel' must be right both from the point of view of the printing impression and the strength and quality of the type-metal in which the type will be cast. With these limitations and considerations in mind, the punch-cutter is at liberty to cut letters of any shape that pleases him or the designer; and if the punch-cutter and the designer are the same person, so much the better. The technical exigencies of punch-cutting being understood, the problems confronting the punch-cutter are lettering problems and typographical problems — what are good letters, and what are good kinds of letters for books, for newspapers, for advertisements . . . ?

¶ Until recent years all letter punches were hand cut, and the printing types derived from them, especially the faces cut before the industrial era, i.e. before the divorce of the designer from the workman, before the workman had become intellectually irresponsible and the designer technically incapable, show a liveliness and variety otherwise unattainable. Moreover, pantographic enlargement or reduction is with hand cutting impossible, and each size of type has to be cut as though it were a new design.

¶ Punch-cutting by machine involves substantially the following procedure: the designer, according to his experience and skill, draws the letters to be cut to an enlarged size (say one to two inches high). The drawing is then again enlarged, by reflecting it through a lens on to a sheet of paper, to about twelve inches high. A draughtsman traces round the enlarged reflection, and the drawing made is laid flat & the line refined according to the draughtsman's discretion, or that of his overseer, with the help of 'french' curves. The refined drawing is then placed under a pantograph, and while the same draughtsman or another traces the pencil end of the pantograph round the drawing the other end

is cutting a sharp groove in a thin layer of wax laid
on a metal bed. When the tracing is complete the
wax slab is taken out and the wax removed, by the
same or yet another draughtsman, from between
the cut grooves, leaving a wax letter lying in relief
on the metal bed. This wax letter is then placed in
an electric bath & copper is electrically deposited
on it. The electrotyping is of course in charge of
another specialist. The wax is then melted out and
a copper matrix of the letter remains ; from this a
'positive' is made, & this is the 'pattern' : it is usually
about four or five inches high. The pattern is then
placed in the punch-cutting machine. This works
on the same pantographic principle. The operator
in charge of it traces round the pattern with the
pencil end of the machine, & the cutting end cuts
the punch to whatever size is required — large or
small from the same pattern. The cutter is designed
to cut the punch with a suitable bevel, more or less
as the hand cutter would do it. If a slight alteration
is required in the punch after it comes out of the
machine, this can be done by hand provided it only
involves cutting away from and not adding to the
punch, & provided that there is someone available
with the required skill. After the punch is cut the

making of the matrix & the casting of the type are
the same whether for hand cut punches or those
cut by the machine, tho' either of these processes
can be done with or without machinery. Mechanical casting appliances offer a higher average of
accuracy, and this is considered of paramount importance by some printers and publishers.

¶ Obviously the great if not the only advantage of
mechanical punch-cutting is that once the pattern
has been made you can cut punches much more
rapidly than it can be done by hand, & that a whole
series of types, from 5 or 6 point up to 72 point, can
be cut from the same pattern. Thus new designs and
all the different sizes can be placed on the market
much more rapidly &, it is hoped, more profitably.

¶ On the face of it, of course, there seems to be no
limit to the powers of the punch-cutting machine ;
anything for which a 'pattern' can be made can be
cut ; & a pattern can be made from anything which
can be drawn by the designer. So the scope of the
machine appears unlimited, at least to its owners.
There are, however, very serious though ill-defined
limits ; for the multiple processes through which
the design has to go in the course of the production
of the punch would be a serious hindrance to the

accurate reproduction of the design, even if all the young ladies & all the young men employed were themselves in full intellectual sympathy with the designer. But this is necessarily far from being the case. Enlargement operators, pantograph operators, pattern makers, electrotypers and machine operators are all necessarily completely tame and dependent upon their overseers. Such interest as they have in the business, apart from the fact that it serves to bring in an honest living, necessarily tends to be that of conscientious machine-minders, interested more in the good working of their machine than in the intellectual quality of the product. It is difficult enough for the designer to draw a letter ten or twenty times as large as the actual type will be and at the same time in right proportion; it requires very great experience and understanding. It is quite impossible for a set of more or less tame employees, even if the local art school has done its poor best for them, to know what a letter enlarged a hundred times will look like when reduced to the size of the intended type. And when the design is in the least degree fanciful or subtle these difficulties are infinitely increased.

¶ It is abundantly clear, therefore, that while the

apparent powers of the machine punch-cutting
process are unlimited, its actual powers are limited to the production of only the most simple and
demonstrably measurable kinds of letters. There
is, however, a large field for the simple & measurable, and it will soon be clear, even to the owners
of punch-cutting machinery, still more to book
publishers and designers of letters, that, as in architecture, furniture making and the making of all
mechanically manufactured articles, an absolute
simplicity is the only legitimate, because the only
respectable, quality to be looked for in the products
of industrialism.

## 5. OF PAPER AND INK

¶ As to paper, it seems to be generally admitted that the kind called, and to some extent properly called, 'hand made' is the best, if only because the most durable. Of this there are, according to the sort of mould used in the making, two kinds, the 'laid' (made in a mould formed of fine metal wires running longitudinally, with stronger transverse wires at considerably greater intervals), and the 'wove' (made in a mould of woven metal fabric). In this distinction there are two things to be noted; first, that a hand made wove paper can be manufactured only in a society which is also equipped for the production of the fabric of which the mould is made (and hence its appearance comparatively late in the history of paper making); and secondly that the distinction applies as a real distinction only to hand made papers. Your machine made paper is naturally wove, & the imitation of the wire-lines is simply by way of extra adornment.

¶ Hand made paper is made in various standard sizes; it is best to use that which naturally folds to the size of book required without cutting (though, of course, the natural rough edge of the sheet may

g

be trimmed off. The leaves of books so trimmed are
more easily turned over, & dust does not so easily
get in between them — tho' this may equally well
be considered as so much nonsense); for a sheet of
good paper is in a certain way venerable; it is natural to fold it; to cut it unnecessarily is shameful.
¶ There are innumerable sorts of machine made
papers. The most durable are those anomalously
called 'mould made', for these, like the hand made
papers, are made from rag. But mould made papers
are not so durable as the hand made, as their fibre is
not so intricately crossed. ¶ Paper is to the printer
as stone is to the sculptor, one of the raw materials
of his trade. The handicraftsman will naturally prefer the hand made, as the sculptor will naturally
prefer the natural to the artificial stone. Birds of a
feather flock together, & handicraftsmen naturally
consort with their own kind. Similarly the industrialist will naturally prefer machine made paper
as being more consonant with the rest of his outfit.
And machine made paper is perfectly good material
so long as it is not made to imitate the appearance
of the hand made. Machine made paper should be
as smooth as possible, and may, of course, be cut &
trimmed ad libitum, as it is not in any way venerable

in itself. It should be smooth because there is no reason why it should be rough, & smoother paper enables the best results to be obtained from power press printing. It is not giving the machine or the machine-minder a fair chance if rough papers and imitation hand made papers be used. Even the hand press printer prefers smooth paper (unless he be that kind of dam-fool who thinks that all smooth hand made things are immoral), just as the sculptor prefers stone free from natural vents and shells and flints; but unless he enters the foreign world of industrialism, and that involves him in other & countless troubles, he will prefer the hand made in spite of its comparative roughness. Moreover, the roughness of hand made paper, though it increases the difficulty of perfectly even printing, requires more impression, and must normally be damped before use, has a certain virtue to the touch and the eye, just as shells and flints in natural Portland stone, though annoying to the sculptor in as much as they make carving difficult, give a certain virtue to the stone which the dead evenness of cement has not.

¶ The printer cannot make his own press or his own paper. The making of printing presses and paper making are necessarily separate trades. But the hand press printer should make his own ink, as the painter should make his own paints. Ink is not a raw material. Oils and pigments are the raw material of ink; patience in grinding is the only virtue required in the craftsman. Of patience there is this to be said. To be patient is to suffer. By their fruits men know one another, but by their sufferings they are what they are. And suffering is not merely the endurance of physical or mental anguish, but of joy also. A rabbit caught in a trap may be supposed to suffer physical anguish: but it suffers nothing else. The man crucified may be supposed to suffer physical & mental anguish, but he suffers also intense happiness and joy. The industrialist workman is often simply as a rabbit in a trap; the artist is often as a man nailed to a cross. In patience souls are possessed. No lower view of the matter will suffice. ¶ But the question of colour must be considered. Even black can be made in a variety of tints, & the use of red and blue and other colours is not a quite simple matter. Traditional uses are safe guides, but fancy intelligently curbed has also its legitimate places. Here again the question is vastly more complicated for those who by inclination or necessity employ industrial methods and the products of industrialism. The factory is able to supply coloured inks in an enormous variety, good & bad ; the publisher and the printer may well be bewildered and be under the necessity of giving much time to the study of the chemical properties of pigments and oils in relation to the innumerable kinds & qualities of machine made papers. The imp who presides over the minds of those who invent 'labour-saving' devices & machinery may well smile to see the complications and worry such inventions bring in their train. ¶ For the handicraftsman, who does not concern himself much with saving labour (except in so far as the avoidance of waste may be called saving ; and every man will have his personal gadgets by which he helps himself in his job), life is much simpler. For him there are not innumerable sorts of paper, type and ink. There is possibly only one sort of paper, one fount of type and, as he makes his ink himself, there is only one sort of ink & two or three different colours. And, paradoxical though it may seem, his legitimate personal fancy has therefore even greater scope than is the case with those who are surrounded to the point of bewilderment by a complicated variety of possible choices. When you say 'black' to a printer in 'big business' the word is almost meaningless, so innumerable are its meanings. To the craftsman, on the other hand, black is simply the black he makes — the word is crammed with meaning; he knows the stuff as well as he knows his own hand. And it is the same with his red and blue. Therefore he can play with colour — as a child can play with a few wooden soldiers and yet would be unable to make up even the simplest games if his nursery floor were completely covered with the leaden armies of Gamage's emporium.

¶ Nevertheless, fancy plays a much less important part in work than reason. The good man is a reasonable man, and the good work is a reasonable work. In typography the use of colour is a reasonable and not a fancy matter, & as every extra colour involves an extra printing, the expense alone places a curb upon the exuberance of the craftsman. ¶ The traditional use of red for the commentary and ritual directions in ecclesiastical books and for the initial letters of more important passages is a reliable precedent where the customer is able to pay for it. At the present time only a few rich enthusiasts are prepared for such expense, with the consequence that such rubricating is only done in books printed for what may be called a luxury market. Rubricating has therefore lost its basis in reason and has become enfeebled fancy work. ¶ Such considerations do not, of course, concern the producers of books in masses, but they are of importance outside the industrial world, and it might be well to consider whether the reasonable use of colour is not as attractive as the often unreasonable use of engraved illustrations and decorations, and, moreover, no more expensive. Reasonableness is the first necessity, the basis of all good; and if this is true of plain printing, much more is it true when the printer's aim is to produce not the useful only but that which is delightful also.

¶ It is obvious that, with letters of different widths and words of different lengths, it is not possible to get a uniform length in all the lines of words on a page. But by sacrificing even spacing between letters and words short lines can be made to fill out to the same length as long ones. When the measure, i.e. the width of a page, is very wide in proportion to the size of type to be used, the sacrifice of even spacing is not noticeable; on the other hand when the measure is very narrow unevenness of spacing becomes obvious. Now uneven spacing is in itself objectionable — more objectionable than uneven length of lines, which is not in itself objectionable. We make no objection to uneven length of lines in blank verse or in a handwritten or typewritten letter. On the other hand, uneven length of line in a page of prose is not in itself desirable.

¶ A very wide measure is objectionable because it involves too much movement of the eye & head in reading, & also because unless the lines be separated by wide spaces (leads), there is danger of doubling, i.e. reading the same line twice or even three times.

¶ A very narrow measure, i.e. narrow in relation

to the type, is objectionable because the phrases and words are too cut up. Practised readers do not read letter by letter or even word by word, but phrase by phrase. It seems that the consensus of opinion favours an average of 10-12 words per line. But a ten-word line is a short one from the point of view of the compositor, i.e. with such a short line even spacing is impossible unless equality of length be sacrificed — or, vice versa, equality of length cannot be obtained without the sacrifice of even spacing. But even spacing is of more importance typographically than equal length. Even spacing is a great assistance to easy reading; hence its pleasantness, for the eye is not vexed by the roughness, jerkiness, restlessness and spottiness which uneven spacing entails, even if such things be reduced to a minimum by careful setting. It may be laid down that even spacing is in itself desirable, that uneven length of lines is not in itself desirable, that both apparently even spacing and equal length of lines may be obtained when the measure allows of over fifteen words to the line, but that the best length for reading is not more than 12 words, & that therefore it is better to sacrifice actual equality of length rather than evenness of spacing, though a measure of compromise is possible so that

apparent evenness of spacing be obtained without
unpleasant raggedness of the right-hand edge. In
other words, working with the 10–12 word line
you can have absolute even spacing if you sacrifice
equal length, but as this will generally entail a very
ragged right-hand edge, the compositor may compromise and, without making his spacing visibly
uneven, he can so vary the spaces between words
in different lines as to make the right-hand edge not
unpleasantly uneven. In any case it is clear that the
10–12 word line and even spacing between words
are in themselves of real & paramount importance,
while the equality of length of lines is not of the
same importance, and can be obtained in a page of
10–12 word lines only by the sacrifice of more important things. In fact, equal length of lines is of its
nature not a sine qua non; it is simply one of those
things you get if you can : it satisfies our appetite
for neat appearance, a laudable appetite, but has
become somewhat of a superstition; and it is generally obtained at too great a sacrifice. A book is
primarily a thing to be read, and the merely neat
appearance of a page of type of which all the lines
are equal in length is a thing of no very great value
in itself; it partakes too much of the ideas of those

who regard books as things to be looked at rather
than read. It is the same sort of superstition as that
according to which all Christian churches should
be 'gothic'; it is a medievalism. But whereas the
medieval scribe obtained his neat square page by
the use of a large number of contractions (by this
means words were made on the average very much
shorter; and obviously short words are more easily
fitted in than long ones) & by the frank use of line-
fillings — i.e. he boldly filled up a short line with an
ornamental flourish or illuminated device — the
modern printer obtains his square page only by the
sacrifice of one of the most important constituents
of readableness, even spacing between words.
Moreover, however neat and square the medieval
page looked, it was not actually so; the scribe always allowed a slight give & take; in fact his methods
were both humane and rational. The modern printer's methods are, of course, not expected to be humane; his irrationality is the more to be deplored,
¶ Appeal to the precedent of the first printed books
is not relevant in this matter of even spacing between
words, or of equality in length of lines; for the early
printers admittedly did no more than imitate what
seemed to them to be the more important parts of

medieval practice without criticism, & were more concerned with their marvellous new power of multiplying books than with questions of typographic rationality. Moreover, the common practice of contraction, also inherited from the medieval scribe, helped still further; & it would be a good thing typographically if, without any reliance upon medieval or incunabulist precedent, modern printers allowed a more frequent use of contractions. The absurd rule that the ampersand (&) should only be used in 'business titles' must be rescinded, & there are many other contractions which a sane typography should encourage.

¶ Another matter, closely connected with even spacing & complementary to it, is the question of close spacing. We have become accustomed to wide gaps between words, not so much because wide spacing makes for legibility as because the Procrustean Bed called the Compositor's Stick has made wide spacing the easiest way out of the difficulty caused by the tyrannical insistence upon equal length of lines. But reasonably close spacing is in itself a desirable thing. Provided that words are really distinct from one another, they should be set as close as possible. Distinctness assumed, closeness makes for that continuous flow which is essential to pleasant reading ; and pleasant reading is the compositor's main object. ¶ Here, of course, it is obvious that by coupling the word 'pleasant' with the word 'reading' we are inviting much controversy. The readable may seem to be a measurable quality, verifiable by eyesight tests & rational exposition; and this may be so; but the pleasantly readable is obviously a much more difficult matter, and involves consideration of the whole business of human loves and hates. This cannot be altogether escaped, and the printer must simply do his best to steer a good course among conflicting temptations. On the other hand, the industrialist will simply do what his customers demand. His work will reflect their quality even more than his, and that quality, at its best, will be what strict utility compels, and, at its worst, what the foolish sensuality of undisciplined minds will swallow. On the other hand the responsible artist, the printer who elects to stand outside industrialism, who regards the job of printing as a sculptor regards the job of stone-carving, or a village blacksmith the job of working iron, regards himself & his customer as sharing a joint enterprise, namely, the production of good books; and the terms good, lovely, pleasant, beautiful, mean for them not merely what will sell, or what can, by cunning advertisement, be made to sell, but what the widest culture & the strictest discipline can make them mean. The discovery, then, of what is meant by 'pleasantly readable' involves more than questions of eye-strain, important tho' that question is; it involves first and last a consideration of what is holy. Here indeed we are outside the bounds of the industrial world and all its advertised humility. Outside that world the term holy loses its exclusively moral significance; it ceases to mean simply ecclesiastical legality or devotion to social 'uplift'; it means what is reasonable no less than what is desirable, the true no less than t..e good. To discover the 'pleasantly readable' the printer & his customer must discover the bounds of the virtue of haste (how far is mere quickness of reading desirable?), the bounds of the virtue of fancifulness (what are the limits beyond which legitimate self-expression becomes indecent self-advertisement?) and other such lesser things. Above all they must collaborate to discover what is really pleasant in human life.

# 7. THE INSTRUMENT

¶ The printing press was invented, we are told, in order that books might be multiplied more quickly and cheaply than could be done by handwriting. Further, we are asked to believe, the early printers were so obsessed by the desire to serve their fellow men by the spread of literature that they had no thought to spare for the business of printing as a good kind of work in itself. And further, it is suggested, the invention of the printing press was inspired by precisely the same ideas and motives as inspire the invention of 20th century machinery; that the 'hand' press is in essence the same kind of machine as the 'power' press, and that printing in the fifteenth century was as much 'mass' production as it is in the twentieth.

¶ Whatever may be said as to the motives of our forefathers (and we must beware of the common fault of historians of seeing the past in terms of the present), it is certainly true that printing is quicker than handwriting, and that the world is served by the spread of literature — though it is not at all certain that it is served well. But, on the other hand, it is not in the least probable that the early printers had no eye for good printing or thought of printing as an inferior way of reproducing lettering. It is not true that a hand operated printing press is essentially the same as one automatically fed and operated by what they call 'power', any more than it is true to say that a hand loom is essentially the same kind of machine as a power loom. It is not a proper use of words to call the work of Caxton 'mass' production; and least of all is it true to say that the early printers were simply men of business.

¶ Here we may content ourselves with the following affirmations : 1. The printing press is a tool for making prints better, as well as quicker, than it can be done by pressing with the unaided hand. The press, whether the pressure be applied by means of levers, screws or rollers, is not simply suitable but indispensable. 2. Writing may be all that calligraphers say of it, & printed lettering is neither better nor worse; it is simply a different kind of thing. Good printing has its own kind of goodness; the motives of its inventors do not concern us. 3. The service rendered to the world by printers is best talked about by those who are served. The printer had better confine his attention to the well doing of what he wants to do or is asked to do, namely to print. When the ser-

vant brags about his services it is probable that he
is stealing the spoons.

¶ Just as some young men want to be engine driv-
ers, others to be stone carvers, & others 'something
in the city', so some want to be printers. What kind
of press should such be advised to procure? Assuming that by printing they mean letterpress printing,
and by printer they mean the man doing the actual
job of setting type and taking prints therefrom (i.e.
assuming that they do not mean simply employing
men to produce printing under their direction), then
there is no sort of doubt that the best sort of tool for
the purpose is one operated by a hand lever. This tool
gives the maximum of control with the minimum of
distraction. It is most important that the workman
should not have to watch his instrument, that his
whole attention should be given to the work. A sculptor does not see his hammer and chisel when he is
carving, but only the stone in front of him. Similarly the hand press printer can give his whole attention to inking & printing, and hardly see his press.
It is far otherwise with the automatically fed power
press. Here the printer becomes little more than a
watcher of his instrument, a machine-minder. If he
be conscientious he will from time to time take a
h

print from the accumulating pile and see whether
it is up to the standard set by his overseer; but his
main attention must be given to the machine to see
that it is running smoothly. Thus with power printing the printer is inevitably a different kind of man
from the hand press printer, and the work done is
also of a different kind. It is not a question whether
machine work be better or worse than hand work —
both have their proper goodness — it is simply a
matter of difference. There are some who aver that
between good machine printing and good hand
printing there is no visible difference, and certainly none worth mentioning. This may very well be
so in particular cases; for the craftsman and the
mechanic often imitate one another. Such & such
a hand press printer may be able to produce work
of such dead accuracy that you would think that it
had been done by mechanics. Such and such a firm
of machine printers may, by careful study of the best
museum examples, be able to produce works which,
though printed in the 20th century, have all the appearance of having been printed in the 18th. Nevertheless, it remains obvious that the general style of
mechanically produced work is different & violently different from the style of that produced by hand;

that the proper and characteristic work of the 20th century bears little likeness to that of the 15th; that industrialism demands different men and produces different things.

¶ In spite of occasional jibes & sneers our argument, then, is not at all that things made by machinery are bad things, or that the handicraftsman is the only kind of man that merits salvation. The industrialist is very welcome to all the credit he can get as a servant of humanity. The time has come when the handicraftsman should cease altogether either to rail at him or envy him. Let each go his own road. The handicraftsman must see that if a million people want the Daily Mail on their breakfast tables it is no affair of his, for he cannot possibly supply them. On the other hand the man of business should be the first to admit that if handicraftsmen can still make a living by printing, they are welcome to do so. The industrialist makes no claim to produce works of art; he does so nevertheless — when he is not imitating the art works of the past. The artist makes no claim to serve his fellow men; nevertheless he does so — when he is not wholly led astray by the notion that art is self-expression or the expression of emotion. The man of business will rightly and properly employ industrial methods (so long as men will submit to them) and machinery (so long as he can procure it). The artist will naturally confine himself to such tools as he can control with his hands.

¶ As the machine demands in the operative a virtue of the will (conscientiousness & good will) or a sharp eye in the overseer, before the mechanical product can secure the technical perfection which is not only proper to the machine but its chief reason for existence, so the response of the craftsman's tool to the control of his hands demands in him a corresponding virtue. But this virtue is one of the mind, judgement. Those are in error, accordingly, who suppose that when the craftsman strives after technical excellence he is emulating the machine standard. And those are even more grievously mistaken who suppose that if the craftsman neglect his responsibility to exercise good judgement and skill in the actual performance of his work, the consequent lack of uniformity (in the colour of his pages or the weight of his impression) will give to his work the vitality or liveliness which is characteristic of hand work.

¶ It may be said of all printers that their job is to reproduce on paper the exact face of the letters which they have set into pages. This face is of a definite, constant and measurable size and shape; with any one press and any one paper there is a right & exact quantity of ink & pressure necessary to reproduce that face without either exaggeration or diminution. When the power printer has found this he has simply to let the machine run on, & 'mind' it to ensure that it run regularly. When the hand printer has found his ink and pressure combination he has constantly to exercise his judgement and manual skill lest his sheets become either too pale or too black. Both sorts of printers aim at evenness, & both are to be blamed if they fail to achieve it. But there is this to be observed: that, in the event, they will be found to have produced different qualities of evenness. The press & method of inking, & sometimes the paper, which the craftsman uses are such that the colour of his work, at its best, is balanced on the very razor edge of accuracy. On either side his tools force on him a very slight margin, so that he is as a tight-rope walker whose deliberate balance gives a different delight from that of the mechanical gyroscope. On the other hand, the power printer, who has not to consider the trifling inconstancies which are inseparable from any hand-operated tool, can achieve a dead level of uniformity in which there is not the smallest apparent variation. Nor is it unreasonable that this perfection should be barren & motionless. While good work, accordingly, from either world should be praised with different praise, it is unreasonable for the craftsman to mistake the shame of vague press-work for the glory of his more humane and livelier method of work.

## 7. THE BOOK

¶ The world of 1931 reads daily news-sheets like that one called the Daily Mail; it is brought up on them; it both produces them & is formed by them. We may take it that the Daily Mail represents the kind of mind that we have got, and in all kinds of subtle ways books are expected to conform to the Daily Mail standard. Legibility is what the Daily Mail reader finds readable; good style is what he finds good; the beautiful is what pleases him.

¶ Makers of books, therefore, who refuse this rather low standard are compelled to efface personal idio-syncrasy & to discover, if it be possible, the real roots of good book-making, just as St. Benedict in the 6th century, confronted by the decayed Roman society, was compelled to discover the roots of good living. Good book-making, good living — that is to say not what you or I fancy, but what the nature of books and the nature of life really demand.

¶ It is all very well for the men of commerce, the commercial people, to brag about themselves as servants of humanity & of the human mind. They say grandly enough that a book is a thing to be read, implying that a book is not a picture to hang on a nail. But this grand air of serving one's fellow men, putting aside a modicum of hypocrisy, does not carry us very far unless we know by whom books are to be read. The standard of readableness is dependent upon the standard of the reader, & the standard of book-making upon the standards of those who make them and of those for whom they are made. Books made by & for unreasoning people may well be expected to conform to unreasonable standards. ¶ It is necessary to point out these facts because many who write typographical criticism seem to think that the business of making books has proceeded steadily from worse to better ever since the invention of printing; they take no account of the steadily increasing pressure of commercialism. Whether we approve or disapprove of the methods of modern commercialism (& we have never denied that many great powers & innumerable small conveniences have been conferred upon us by the wedding of experimental science and capitalist bookkeeping — the abolition of 'double-entry' would paralyse modern trade as much as the abolition of paper would paralyse modern architecture) we cannot deny that the character of those modern things which are not curbed by the strictest utilitarianism

is that of materialist triumph tempered by fancifulness and sloppiness, & that they are altogether without grace either in the physical or spiritual senses of
the word.

¶ A book is a thing to be read — we all start with
that — and we will assume that the reader is a sensitive as well as a sensible person. Now, the first
thing to be noticed is that it is the act of reading &
the circumstances of that act which determine the
size of the book and the kind of type used; the reading, not what is read. A good type is suitable for any
and every book, and the size of a book is regulated
not by what is in it but by the fact that it is read held
in the hand (e.g. a novel), or at a table (e.g. books of
history or reference with maps or other necessarily
large illustrations), or at a desk or lectern (e.g. a mis-
sal or a choir book), or kept in the pocket (e.g. a
prayer book or a travellers' dictionary). ¶ On the
contrary some hold that size of book and style of
type sh'ld be specially chosen for every book; that
such & such a size is suitable for Shakespeare; such
and such for Mr. Wells's novels, such and such for
Mr. Eliot's poems; that the type suitable for one is
not suitable for another; that elegant poetry should
have elegant type, & the rough hacked style of Walt

Whitman a rough hacked style of letter; that reprints
of Malory should be printed in 'Black Letter' and
books of technology in 'Sans-serif'. There is a certain plausibility in all this, & even a certain reasonableness. The undignified typography of the Daily
Mail Year Book is certainly unsuitable for the Bible;
a fine italic might be suitable for Milton but unsuitable for 'Tono-Bungay'; sans-serif may be suitable
for a translation of Jean Cocteau but might be unsuitable for a pocket prayer book. And as to size: it
is impossible to print the Bible on too grand a scale,
but third-rate verse might look and be absurd in a
book requiring a lectern to hold it. Nevertheless,
the reasonable producer of books starts with the
principle that it is the reading, not the reading matter, which determines the size of book and style of
type; the other considerations come in only as modi-
fying influences. In planning a book the first questions are: who is going to read this, and under what
circumstances?

¶ If, then, there are normally four sizes of books,
it would seem that there sh'ld be four sizes of type.
A pocket book demands small type, say 8 point, for
reasons of space. A book held in the hand demands
type of about 10 or 12 point on account of the length

of the human arm and the normal power of human
eyesight, assuming a normally legible type. Table
books & lectern books, normally read further from
the eye, demand types of still larger sizes, say 14 or
18 point or over. But the sizes of types named here
are not binding on anybody; it is only the principle
we are concerned with. ¶ The proportions of books
were formerly determined by the sizes of printing
papers. These were always oblong in shape (probably because this was the shape most easily handled
by the makers, or, perhaps, because the skins of
animals used for writing on in medieval times are
of this shape, and so books followed suit) & when
folded in half and in half again and so on, made a
narrow folio, a wide quarto, a narrow octavo, &c.
But with the machine made papers now almost
universally used these proportions are only retained
by custom, the width of the web of paper and the
direction of the grain being the only determining
factors. Books printed on machine made paper can,
these factors understood, be of any shape that pleases
you. And thus the commercial book designer is, to
a greater degree than his predecessor, released from
the thraldom of any considerations but that of what
will sell.

¶ As to what does or should sell, we may say that
the things which should form the shape & proportions of the page are the hand and the eye; the hand
because books of wide proportions are unwieldy to
hold; and the eye because lines of more than 10–12
words are awkward to read. (With longer lines, set
solid, i.e. without leads between them, there is difficulty in following from one line to the next, &, even
if the type be leaded, a long line necessitates a distinctly felt muscular movement of the eye and, in
extreme cases, of the head.) As to the height of a
page, this again is governed by the needs of hand &
eye; a very tall page necessitates either a distinct
movement of the neck of the reader or a changing
of the angle at which the book is held in the hand,
& such things are simply a nuisance. It may be that
there are other considerations than those of physical
convenience which have helped to determine the
normal octavo page; it may be that such a proportion is intrinsically pleasing to the human mind. It
is, however, sufficient for us to see that there is a
physical reasonableness in this proportion, and we
may safely leave the discovery of other reasons to
professional æstheticians.

¶ The shape of the page being given, it remains to

discover the best proportions for the lines & mass
of type printed upon it. Here again physical considerations are a sufficient guide. Two things are to
be thought of : the type & the margins. Let us consider the margins first. The inner margin exists simply to separate a page from the one opposite to it,
and need be no wider than is enough to keep the
printed words clear of the bend of the paper where
it is sewn in binding. The top margin, again, needs
only to be sufficiently wide to isolate the type from
the surrounding landscape of furniture and carpets
(just as a 'mount' or frame is used by painters to
isolate a picture from wall paper, &c.). On the other
hand, the outer and bottom margins need more
width than is required for mere isolation, for it is
by these margins that the book is held in the hand ;
enough must be allowed for thumbs, and the bottom margins need more than the side or outer ones.
These physical considerations being allowed for,
we may now consider the margins in relation to
one another, & it will be seen at once that, taking
one page at a time, i.e. half the 'opening', slightly
more must be allowed to the top margin than is required for mere isolation ; for if you make the top
and inner margins equally narrow, the outer mar-

gin wide and the bottom still wider, the text will appear to be being pushed off the top. We may say then that the general rule should be: a narrow inner margin, a slightly wider top margin, an outer margin at least double the inner, and a bottom slightly wider than the others; the exact proportions being left to the judgement of the printer. It is to be noted that unless the outer margin be at least double the inner the two inner margins, seen together when the book is opened, will appear to be pushing the text outwards off the page.

¶ With a normal octavo page of 5 inches wide and $7\frac{1}{2}$ inches high, & supposing that we allow margins as follows: inner, $\frac{1}{2}$ inch; top, $\frac{3}{4}$; outer 1; & bottom, $1\frac{1}{6}$; we shall get a type page $3\frac{1}{2}$ inches wide by $5\frac{2}{3}$ inches high (i.e. 34 lines of pica type, 12 pt., set solid). This allows for a line of an average length of 10–12 words in pica, & pica is a good ordinary size for a book held in the hand. Obviously these dimensions may be varied slightly without destroying the rationality or normality of the page, & type slightly larger or smaller than pica (12 pt.) can be used without extravagance or loss of legibility; though it is obvious that, for reasons of physical convenience, a variation that entails a lengthening

of the line to more than 1 2 or 1 3 words is a variation
in a direction less commendable than one that entails
a shortening of the line. The dimensions given may
therefore be taken as a norm.

¶ The title page should be set in the same style of
type as the book and preferably in the same size.
The unfortunate printers who regard the title page
as the only source of interest in an otherwise dull
job are the miserable descendants of those scribes
who knowing and even appreciating the glory of
the books they wrote out naturally gave a glorious
beginning to them. The title of a book is merely the
thing to know it by; we have made of the title page
a showing-off ground for the printers & publishers.
A smart title page will not redeem a dully printed
book any more than a smart cinema will redeem a
slum. ¶ The title of the book & its author's name
must be given somewhere. They may be placed at
the top of the first page of the book, or at the top
of the contents page, if any, or on a blank page left
for the purpose. ¶ The addition of the publisher's
name & address has the sanction of long establishment & the compulsion of the law; but, apart from
the needs of advertisement, such things should, like
the name & sign of the printer, be placed at the end of

the book where indeed they naturally come. In the industrial world, however, the necessity of advertisement is felt to be paramount, & the typographic exigencies have been compromised. It would be better to be frank about this &, to avoid the present confusion between the needs of the book & those of the publisher, to place the publisher's name & address & sign on a page by themselves preceding the title or opening page of the book proper. Thus on opening the book the first printed page would give the bare title & the advertisement of the publisher, the next would give the title, sub-title if any or list of contents &, continuing on the same page or at the top of the next, the beginning of the book itself. By this arrangement the legitimate demands of both printer and publisher would be met.

¶ The bulk of the book is also a thing to be considered. By increasing the margins and leading the type the number of pages will be increased, and this may be desirable on various grounds. For instance where great legibility is required the leading of the type is helpful; or where the text is short and the book consequently a very thin one, the increase of margins and the use of leads may give that bulk to the book which habit has made pleasant. Even the business of bookselling makes its legitimate demands; books commend themselves to buyers by their weight, bulk and size as well as by their titles or their typography, and this is not entirely foolish. Books have got to be handled as well as read, and they have got to stand on shelves. Nevertheless there is no occasion to go to extremes in this matter, & it is as foolish to make a thick book of a short story as it is, by small type and cramped margins, to make one volume of a book which is properly two.

¶ As to binding : the continental practice of issuing books in sheets, or simply sewn with a paper wrapper, is much to be praised. The English book buyer's insistence on a stiff cover, even for the cheapest books, has been met by the invention or development of the 'case', i.e. a stiff cover which may be applied after the sheets are sewn, and is designed for making in large quantities. The only objection to such cases it that they nearly always retain certain conventional ornamentations which are derived from the 'binding' of former times and are not appropriate to machine made things. For sixpenny novels the work is done from end to end by machine — including the ornaments on the sides and back. For more expensive books some parts of the work

i

are still done by hand, e.g. the pasting of the end-
sheets & the insertion of head bands of parti-coloured
cloth. But except for individual private customers
'binding', i.e. the sewing of the sheets & the lacing
of the whole thing to the cover so that book & cover
are one thing, is not done at all. Doubtless the ordinary products of commercial printing are not suitable
for any other treatment, & while the cry is for cheaper & cheaper books anything but what can be done
by machine is out of the question. Printing done by
machinery on machine made paper may well be
cased in machine made casing, but printing done
by human beings on paper made by human beings
ought to be bound by human beings.

¶ The question arises: how many copies of a book
should be printed? There are several appropriate
answers to this question. The first is: as many as
can be sold; and this is the only answer we shall
consider here. But there are two primary considerations in the selling of anything: (a) the number
of people who can be supposed to desire a thing
because it is desirable in itself; and (b) the number
who can afford to buy it. If all those to whom a
book is desirable can afford to buy it, then the edition is properly limited to 'all those'; but if only a

few can afford to buy it, the edition is properly limited to that few. What is this book? How ought it
to be printed? These things being determined, the
ground is clear for the consideration of the problem
of the number of possible buyers. ¶ It is obvious
that the number of possible buyers of expensive
books is comparatively small. This will always be
so, and rightly. That everybody should be 'rich' is,
in the nature of things, neither possible nor desirable. That everybody should be able to read or even
wish to do so, is extremely doubtful. There is therefore no question of the limited production of expensive books involving any injustice, and, apart
from the efforts of a few earnest enthusiasts, the
production of cheap literature, whether daily newspapers or books, is without doubt the affair not of
those interested in books but of men of business interested in money. They do not ask themselves: how
well can this thing be done? but: how large a market
can we 'tap'? And to this end they have brought into
existence all the manifold powers of machinery &
advertisement — a vicious circle; for the more the
human race is degraded by industrialism, the larger
is the market for inferior articles ; in order to reach
a larger and still larger number of buyers you pro-

duce a lower and still lower quality of goods.

¶ But here we are not concerned with such a problem. Obviously there is only one just cause for the
limitation of an edition, and that is the size of the
market. Provided you are concerned to make books
as well as they can be made — and this not so much
in a spirit of piety (though we do not disdain the
virtue of Prudence) as in a spirit of reasonableness,
for ultimately there is no happiness in a world in
which things are not as good as they can be — the
size of your edition will depend simply upon your
judgement and experience as to the number of possible buyers. And if, owing to the time factor, you
cannot supply in a reasonable time all who would
buy, then you can produce second & third editions.

¶ We may here go into the question of the artificial limitation of numbers in order to capture a
'collectors' market. Properly understood this is a
purely 'business' matter, and the printer whose
first concern is quality is not a man of business. Let
us suppose that both the craftsman and the industrialist have produced as many of their respective
products as they can sell. What further can either
of them do? ¶ The craftsman can introduce into his
workshop a bit of machinery, and, without its be-

ing noticeable to his customers, produce the same number of books more cheaply & therefore more profitably. He will continue to produce the same number, but now, instead of that number being the largest number he can sell, it will be the most profitable number. ¶ The industrialist can introduce into his factory a book designer who has studied in the museums where they store pre-industrial productions, &, by careful watching of the work of 'private' presses and of the market supplied by them, he may produce, at a very considerably higher price than they cost him to make, a 'limited' edition which will make almost as much appeal to collectors as the work of Cobden-Sanderson & his predecessors. This is simply a matter of business. ¶ There are, then, two principles, as there are two worlds. There is the principle of best possible quality, and the principle of greatest possible profit. And there is every sort of compromise between the two. Whether, as seems probable, industrialism win a complete victory, or human nature so far reassert itself as to overthrow industrialism, is not here our concern. For the present we hold simply to the conviction that the two principles and the two worlds can exist side by side, industrialism becoming more

strictly and nobly utilitarian as it recognises its inherent limitations, and the world of human labour,
ceasing any longer to compete with it, becoming
more strictly and soberly humane.

¶ We take lettering 'for granted'. 'Can you read?' is almost the first question we ask a child when we meet it, after its first term at the infants' school ! Letters are signs for sounds, but how A, B, & C come to be signs for the particular sounds they are supposed to signify we seldom consider. Let us briefly go over the history of the letters we use. I don't mean such a history as only the archæologians know ; I mean such a history as is obvious and guessable and common gossip.

¶ I think it is generally agreed that picture writing was the beginning of our lettering. You might wish to communicate something to someone at a distance. If you have no letters or none common both to you & your correspondent, what else can you do but draw a picture? — the language of pictures is common to all. After a time your pictures are used to signify words and not simply things, and as the system develops and communications become more precise, the pictures become simpler and simpler, more & more conventional, and they come to signify single sounds rather than whole words. And the pictures, by now, have ceased to be pictures. They are, by now, hardly recognisable as representations of things ; they are conventional signs, & their pictorial origin is forgotten.

¶ But after centuries of this sort of thing another complication arises. I have only to say the word spelling & everyone will see again before him the spectre which haunted our first schooldays, and which does not leave us in peace even in old age. Spelling is putting letters together to make words ; but these letters have by now ceased to be purely sound symbols. It is no longer possible, even if it ever was, to say that such and such a letter always and everywhere signifies such and such a sound ; and, for example, a combination of the four letters O U G H is used to signify at least seven distinctly and even widely different sounds — 'Though the tough cough and hiccough plough me through, my thought remains clear' and it is this : that it is simply stupid to make pretence any longer that our letters are a reasonable means for rendering our speech in writing or printing.

¶ But it is not only in the matter of spelling that letters are ridiculous. There is another and equally important aspect of the matter. Not only have letters largely ceased to signify the sounds of our language, but the business of writing bears no relation to the business of speaking. There is no correspondence between talking & writing it down. Writing is not written talk; it is a translation of talk into a clumsy & difficult medium which has no relation whatever to the time factor of speech and very little relation to the sound. It is in fact an entirely outworn, decayed and corrupt convention whose chief & most conspicuous character is its monumental witness to the conservatism, laziness and irrationality of men and women.

¶ It will not be supposed that I am moved in this matter by any such absurd notion as that 'time is money'. Nor am I blind to the claims of the pedants — with their long arguments about philology and the value of spelling as a witness to the historical origins of our words. Nor, least of all, am I unaware of the pleasing nature of letters as things to look at or the pleasing nature of the written or printed sheet of Roman, or even medieval lettering. History has a fascination for everyone and the history of language is as interesting as any other. A well printed page, a good inscription or a piece of medieval handwriting are good things to see. Look, for instance, at that extraordinary and truly marvellous manuscript bought recently at a fabulous and absurd figure of money from our worthy and revered friends the Bolshevists — everyone can see it in the excellent collotype reproduction sold at the British Museum for a few pence, & those of you who are not satisfied with the collotype could just as well have gone to Moscow to see the original now that the Soviet steamers and railway trains are organised upon the best capitalist models. I say a good piece of lettering is as beautiful a thing to see as any sculpture or painted picture.

¶ Moreover, although the saying 'time is money' is too difficult for me to understand (and for millions of our fellow countrymen, thrown out of employment by improvements in machinery, with too much time on their hands and practically no money at all, the saying is obviously absurd), all the same I see no reason for wasting time or taking longer on a job than is necessary to do it well. No, in spite of the charms of history, in spite of the allurements of artistry and in spite of the danger of being thought to play into the hands of men of business (and who, confronted by the world which men of business have made, would willingly take that risk?), in spite of these things the balance of argument still seems to be strongly upon the side of revolution.

¶ What is the revolution demanded? Reformed spelling? No, *the abolition of spelling* — the abolition of lettering as we know it altogether. And the thing is easy to accomplish — all that is required is the will to do it — the will informed by the intelligent appreciation of its reasonableness. For what is the remedy? It is plain before our eyes. Nothing is required but that every child shall be taught 'shorthand' at school — not as an optional subject, not as a subject only suitable for those destined or compelled to a commercial career (if indeed, remembering the origin of the word 'career', & its association with medieval tournaments and high adventures, we can call the life of a shorthand clerk a career at all). I say *shorthand* should be taught as a proper subject for all and one of primary importance.

¶ But let us abolish the word *shorthand* — let us call it *phonography* or even simply *writing*. The point of my contention is not that we need a shorter system but a more reasonable one. We need a system in which there is a real correspondence between speech, that is to say the sounds of language, & the means of communication. Why should I think the word *thought* and say the word *thought* and then have the intolerable pain of writing a thing so silly

as  t h o u g h t ?  Those who have had the experience of teaching children to spell & especially
those who have given serious consideration to the
matter will of course immediately understand my
enthusiasm. It is a constant source of exasperation
to those who merely teach, and still more to those
who know that man is (in spite of any appearance
to the contrary) a rational animal, to have the hor-
rid job of marring the budding minds of children by
a set of irrational rules and capricious exceptions.
If we want to train children's memories, let us put
before them something worth remembering. If we
want to teach them to use pens and pencils, let us
teach them drawing. If we want to teach them philology, let us do it orally or by phonography. And if
among our pupils there are budding archæologians,
let them study Roman lettering as we study hieroglyphics.

¶ At any rate the first thing to do is to teach everyone phonography. Whether it be by Pitman's method or another and better one does not matter at
the moment. It is not the absolutely quickest system that we require but, first of all, the most reasonable. Indeed mere speed in shorthand has no longer
even the commercial value it had. The dictaphone

is well on the way to making the use of shorthand commercially unnecessary. Let us abolish from our minds any considerations of mere speed. There is no more reason why the speed of writing should be as great as that of fast speech than there is that the speed of speech should be as great as the speed of fast thought. Think slowly, speak slowly, write slowly; but think the words, speak the sounds and write something which reasonably presents those sounds.

¶ I say again: first teach all the children. And that would be easy. Most schools, especially those in towns, are already equipped with teachers capable of doing the work. One generation of children so brought up would give us a population familiar with words written phonographically — a population which would see as much meaning in a text written phonographically as we of our generation do in texts written in Roman lettering. In very few generations phonography would be venerable and the shapes of its signs endowed with loveliness for us.

¶ If anyone is so sentimental as to worry about beauty, let him take comfort. There is no shape which is intrinsically ugly, no colour, no sound, no smell. A bad smell is simply one which we recognise as harmful or which we associate with harmful things. So also with colours and sounds. The bad colours of our aniline-dyed fabrics are only bad because the human eye is hurt by unrelieved monotony. The colour of the neon light is a good colour in itself; it only nauseates because it is mathematically uniform. Mathematical uniformity is incompatible with the human spirit; and it nauseates also because it reminds us of the unrelieved acquisitiveness of the unfortunate shopkeepers who in our absurd financial chaos cannot persuade us to buy their wretched wares unless they blind and blast our eyes. The sound of the klaxon hurts our ears — it is meant to do so — lest worse befall us. Were it as rare as the screech of the peacock we should like it — at any rate its associations would be more delightful.

¶ So it is with the shapes of things: who would be so foolish as to say that the 'pot-hook' is less beautiful than the 'hanger', that it is less pleasing when seen (for what else but that which pleases when seen can possibly be the beautiful?), and who would say that either 'pot-hooks' or 'hangers' are less beautiful than squares & circles? Such talk is pure nonsense. There are no such things as shapes except the shapes of things, and if the things be good things only fools could deem them ugly. It is not the shapes of gables and lattice windows which are ugly in sham Elizabethan villas, but the downright silliness of all such attempts at putting back the clock — attempts usually made by those practical men of business who think themselves up-to-date. A section of drain pipe is no more ugly than a circle made with compasses. We only think it so because we don't see the circle and only remember the business of drainage.

¶ So there is no earthly, still less any heavenly, reason why phonography should be less beautiful, less pleasing to look at, than Roman inscriptions, medieval manuscripts or the best modern printing. All that is necessary to make phonography beautiful is that men should love it, and if once it became a recognised vehicle of the common language we should soon endow it with loveliness.

¶ And naturally it would soon occur that there would develop three or four or many different forms or adaptations of phonographic symbols. The engraver, the printer, the designer of advertisements, even the tombstone inscription cutter, will all make their characteristic contributions, and no one needs to bother about it beforehand.

¶ And there is one particularly strong argument in

favour of phonography as the common form of writing, and that is that no one will have to scribble as everyone does now. It is true that the shorthand clerk scribbles her shorthand as execrably as other people scribble their longhand — so that none but herself can read what she has written. But that is because she is professionally in a hurry — her living depends upon her ability to write as fast as anyone can speak. There is no such hurry when I write my love letters or my notes to the butcher. There is in fact plenty of time to write shorthand slowly and therefore neatly and legibly.

¶ As things are at present, handwriting has been ruined because everyone is forced to scribble. The only use of handwriting to-day is for the making of personal communications between friends, and in spite of every improvement & cheapening of typewriting machines there will always be a necessity for people to communicate by handwriting. Let such writing be in phonography; then the writing will be a logical presentation of speech, there will be a real time correspondence between speaking & writing, and last of all, but not least, there will be no excuse for bad writing, illegible writing, careless writing, slovenly writing.

¶ It may be urged that in so far as people have to make use of handwritten communications there is a very good case for shorthand or phonography, but that for printed work phonography would have no advantage over the traditional lettering, but this is not so. The printed word has to be set up or composed letter by letter as much as handwritten or typewritten reading matter. Phonographic signs are very considerably fewer in number per word than letters, and a corresponding economy of time and effort would be won if books were printed phonographically instead of in letters.

¶ What I want therefore is, first, some enterprising minister of education who will institute phonography as a compulsory subject in all elementary schools; and, second, some enterprising type-founder who will commission me to design a fount of phonographic symbols.

¶ Let us in conclusion consider the matter on general grounds. Let us consider this matter of reading and writing & printing in relation to our civilisation. What has our civilisation in common with the civilisation of medieval England or that of ancient Rome? Men and women are the same as they always were. Physically and psychologically there's nothing to
k

choose between men and women of to-day & those of the time of Homer. Naturally we suffer from nerves more than our ancestors — but then we have so much more to worry us. Naturally we have diseases they knew not of, but then we live so much less healthily — cooped up in towns & those rows of boxes we call railway trains — the Flying Scotsman is still a row of boxes even though it is dolled up to look like the Strand Palace Hotel. Naturally we are much more clever at mechanics than were our ancestors. But then we have chosen to go in for physics instead of metaphysics. Metaphysics seems nonsense to us & physics seemed nonsense to them.

¶ But inside, underneath, men and women are still mere men and women. Sitting down and talking, eating and drinking, love-making and going to bed — what possible difference is there in these activities to-day from yesterday or a thousand years ago? And our mortal frame! Is it not as mortal as ever? & still it is begotten as it always was and nourished on the same nourishment.

¶ All the same, this is a different civilisation from its predecessors — just as cricket is a different game from football. And as we are now playing a different game from that played by our forefathers before they developed the modern co-operative system which we call industrialism — I call it 'co-operative' because, as I am informed, it takes the co-operation of 18 men to mind the machine which makes a pin and the co-operation of eighteen thousand men to mind the machines which make the pin-making machine which the pin-makers mind, and, further, it takes the co-operation of many more men and women to pack, transport, advertise, keep the accounts and sell the pin when made — so that now we may say the making of anything involves the co-operation of practically everybody, and if that is not a co-operative state, what is? — I say as we are now playing a different game from that of our forefathers we should be annoyed to be compelled to play it according to obsolete rules and to use signs and symbols which were developed and nourished according to the necessities of a game we have ceased to play.

¶ The writing of language in former times was the affair of small and isolated scriptoria. Readers were few and leisured. The idea was entirely absent that every man, woman and child should be able to read & write. They held it sufficient that everyone should merely talk. Now things are quite different. There is first of all a national system of compulsory literary education paid for by national taxation. Good or bad, schools are neither small nor isolated. Nothing could be easier than for an enlightened minister in Whitehall to compel all children to learn Volapük or Chinese.

¶ Moreover the business of printed lettering has now, under the spur of commercial competition, got altogether out of hand and gone mad. There are now about as many different varieties of letters as there are different kinds of fools. I myself am responsible for designing five different sorts of sans-serif letters — each one thicker and fatter than the last because every advertisement has to try and shout down its neighbours. And as there are a thousand different sorts of fancy lettering so there are many too many different sorts of types for reading in books — all of them copies and resuscitations and re-hashes and corruptions of the printing types designed in pre-industrial days — none of them designed for modern machine production; & the machines themselves are complicated by every sort of complicated mechanism for producing the appearance of pre-industrial things. You cannot put back the clock — no. But you can at least recognise that a certain amount of time has passed & not pretend that we are still ancient Britons. Lettering has had its day, Spelling, and philology, and all such pedantries have no place in our world. The only way to reform modern lettering is to abolish it.

BORN IN 1882 in Brighton, England, Eric Gill displayed interest and talent in lettering and architecture at an early age. Encouraged by W.R. Lethaby of the Central School of the Arts and Crafts, he began carving letters and attending the classes of Edward Johnston. In 1903 he struck out on his own, beginning his life-long career as a self-employed craftsman.

In 1924 Stanley Morison asked Gill to write about typography for *The Fleuron*. He declined, saying that typography was "not his country." By 1925, however, Gill had started drawing alphabets (one of which was eventually to become Perpetua) as well as formulating the principles later collected in his celebrated "Essay."

Eric Gill was a man of countless talents. By his death in 1940 he had mastered any number of crafts: sculptor, stone carver, engraver, philosopher, and type designer. But at heart he was always a progressive radical, a social reformer whose work always reflected his philosophy, and whose hand always followed his moral convictions.

## An Essay on Typography

was set in Joanna, one of Eric Gill's least used and most
beautiful faces. Probably named after his daughter
Joan, it was first used as a proprietary face at the
printing press Gill ran with René Hague. Unlike Perpetua, which looks as though it were engraved with a
burin, Joanna looks as though it were cut with a
chisel; it is heavier and more monotone in its weight.
It maintains the typical Perpetua forms, but the serifs
are slab sided and the capitals are visibly shorter than
the ascenders. Like Perpetua, the italic is really a sloped
Roman, but it is highly condensed and decidedly calli-
graphic in many of its features. Characterized by an
evenness and density that make it a readable typeface
with a slightly quirky elegance, Joanna deserves wider
use and recognition.

March 1708